Is Jesus A[live?]

The Evidence and [...]

By Jeremy Royal Howard, Ph. D.
Author, *Holman QuickSource Guide to Understanding Jesus*

Is Jesus alive today? You might think it's a foolish question. After all, Jesus was born over 2,000 years ago and His death remains history's most publicized, violent, and infamous execution. Jesus was extraordinary, but even great men do not return from death. Science and everyday experience prove this, and the ancients knew it as surely as we do. On rare occasions a person will cross into the shadows and then come rushing back when a failed heart restarts or when air-starved lungs are emptied of water, but once a body has been mourned over, ceremonially cleaned and clothed, and committed to silent earth, stone chamber, or consuming fire, their tale among the living is over. Nevertheless, for 2,000 years people have held that Jesus returned to life after three days. Even now, in the age of science, more than two billion people worship Jesus as the living God. Some are scientists or scholars; others shine shoes or work the night shift. Some are rich; others are poor. Some reflected deeply on challenges to Christianity before casting their lot with Jesus; others believed without investigating. With one voice this diverse throng testifies that Jesus is alive today. Is this belief credible? What does the evidence say, and why should it matter to you?

The Life and Death of Jesus

Jesus was born under a cloud of suspicion because His mother became pregnant before marriage. Neighbors assumed she had engaged in forbidden relations. Mary knew this was untrue, but how could she admit the truth? Jesus had been conceived by the Holy Spirit, and an angel said He was God's Son. Try telling that to your neighbors! Understandably, she kept quiet even as God granted signs of Jesus' extraordinary identity. At Jesus' birth He disclosed the truth to lowly shepherds. Days later, two aged saints found baby Jesus and shared revelations from God. When Jesus was a toddler, wise men from afar worshipped Him because God told them that He was King of kings. In these moments God identified Jesus as heaven-sent, but this did not smooth His path. In fact, the revelations to the wise men nearly cost Jesus His life, for their worship prompted King Herod to slay all male toddlers in Bethlehem in an attempt to protect his throne from the newborn King. Jesus and His family escaped when an angel urged them to flee to Egypt. Young Jesus evaded death, but opposition always stalked Him.

Sometime in his thirties Jesus began teaching about His identity, His purposes, and His plan to redeem sinful humanity. He performed works of power that displayed His mastery over nature, sickness, and spiritual dark forces. In short, His words and actions testified that He was God in flesh, sent by the Father to bring light, hope, and salvation. He told us to love God above all and renounce our sins. He named Himself as the world's lone hope and said anyone who wishes to be saved from God's judgment against sin must follow Him. Some people found hope in Jesus' message. Others listened with stony ears and rejected Him as a blasphemer and a conjuror of magic.

As Israel languished under Roman rule, the Jews longed for the right to self-governance. Hopes naturally turned toward Messiah, the super-leader whom God had long ago promised to send for His people. The Jews believed Messiah would save them from their troubles, but most did not perceive that their chief troubles were spiritual rather than national, personal rather than political. They longed for a man of war, a battlefield victor who would strike the earth and restore their traditions. They wanted a Messiah who would vindicate them and lead them in revolution, not chasten them and teach them unpopular truths about God and salvation. These mistaken expectations and short-sighted interests form a vital backdrop for understanding why Jesus' teachings and mission were met with disbelief and hostility among Israel's religious authorities.

Jesus did not seek worldly power. His choice spot was among outcasts. Once He gained momentum among common folk with His promise of eternal life, the religious leaders moved to shut Him down. Jesus knew it would come to this. On several occasions He told His disciples that He had come for the purpose of dying at the hands of injustice. The disciples never understood or accepted this. Like other Jews, they could not imagine that God's Messiah would be rejected and killed. Yet Jesus persisted in this plan. He had come to die on behalf of the people, and He never modified His message or purpose. Finally there came the climactic week of the Passover festival. Out of fear that Jesus' followers would incite riot, disdain for Jesus' teachings, and outright jealousy over Jesus' popularity, the religious leaders decided to kill Jesus. When night fell on the eve of Passover, Jesus was routed out of the garden of Gethsemane and put on trial while Jerusalem slept. The Jews lacked the right to execute criminals, and so they worked to convince the Roman governor (Pilate) that Jesus deserved death. Pilate found their case unconvincing, but he granted their wish because Jesus' claims seemingly made Him a threat to Caesar's rule. Consequently, history's lone innocent man was put to death alongside two rebels on a Friday morning. Still, the priests were not satisfied. Jesus had predicted that He would rise from death. Fearing that His disciples might steal the body and thus fabricate a resurrection, the priests asked Pilate to supply a detachment of guards to ward intruders away from the tomb. It is unclear whether Pilate granted the use of Roman soldiers or else bade the Jews use their temple policemen. In any event the Jews sealed the tomb and set a guard. No one could tamper with the site, let alone haul away Jesus' body. Barring an unmistakable miracle, the dead Jesus would remain locked away behind silent stone for the rest of history.

The Resurrection of Jesus

No one who watched Jesus die expected Him to rise from the dead. That is why all but a few of Jesus' followers fled the crucifixion scene or avoided it altogether. For them, the cross meant the end of Jesus' life and all their best hopes. But then Sunday came. At dawn a group of women went to Jesus' tomb. They had watched His interment on Friday. Now they returned, hoping someone would remove the stone so they could perform additional funerary services, which would ensure that their deceased Lord would not produce a stench. The women did not know that guards were posted at the tomb; they had kept indoors during the Sabbath and consequently received no news. As they drew near, the ground began to heave and revolt. Angels descended. They looked like ordinary men except for their dazzling white clothes. One of the angels rolled back the tomb's sealing stone and sat atop it like a battlefield victor astride his slain foe. Death was dead, but it was not the angel's doing. All he had done was reveal a vacant tomb. The resurrection event had already occurred, unmarked by human eye. The dumbfounded guards stayed long enough to see that the tomb was vacant. They had failed. They knew theft was not the cause since they had kept watch. Nevertheless they struck a deal with the priests to cite theft as the explanation for the empty tomb.

Dazed and troubled, some of the women heard from an angel that Jesus had risen. Unsure what to believe, they hastened toward town but met Jesus on the way. They fell at His feet and worshipped, and then obeyed His command to go tell the men. Meanwhile, Mary Magdalene had gone ahead of these women and did not see Jesus. For her, the empty tomb only proved that some dark soul had stolen Jesus' body as a last insult. When she found Peter, she reported that Jesus' body was stolen. Just as the men got charged up at this news, in came the other women. They gave an ecstatic report that mixed poorly with Mary's pessimism. The emotion-packed scene descended into confusion. On one hand Mary reported a theft; on the other hand her late-arriving companions told tales of a living Jesus wandering along the road. Believing none of it but feeling compelled to investigate, Peter ran for the tomb. John followed but soon outpaced Peter. Upon seeing the empty head cloth that lay inside the tomb, John understood that Jesus had risen from the dead. Peter was slower on the uptake. He was amazed at the evidence, but amazement is not belief. For him, much remained unresolved until he saw Jesus for himself later that day. By late evening many of Christ's disciples had seen Him, for He appeared to them as they gathered behind closed doors. Many others saw Jesus in the days and weeks that followed. One by one, doubts were overturned by the overwhelming evidence that Jesus had come back to life.

Examining the Evidence

Since the resurrection of Jesus is the absolute foundation of Christianity, thoughtful persons have asked hard questions about the evidence. Below we examine ten leading arguments for and against Jesus' resurrection.

The Wrong Tomb—Jesus' friends and foes acknowledged that His tomb was empty on Sunday morning. In the aftermath of this discovery, the disciples heralded Jesus' resurrection while nonbelieving priests rigged up a story saying the disciples had stolen His body. The "stolen body" theory was never convincing because the disciples had nothing to gain by stealing the body, hiding it, and then circulating a resurrection story that only caused them to be persecuted by Jews and Romans alike. Clearly Jesus' followers really believed He had vacated His tomb via resurrection. Seeing the force of the empty tomb as evidence for the resurrection, skeptics eventually concocted an alternative explanation. Instead of acknowledging that Jesus' tomb was empty on Sunday morning, some skeptics assert that the bumbling disciples went to the wrong tomb. Failing to realize their mistake, they ran off believing in a resurrected Jesus when in reality He lay dead as ever in a nearby tomb.

Before evaluating this theory, we must note that Jesus' burial site was a matter of public knowledge. The tomb belonged to a man named Joseph who teamed up with Nicodemus and interred Jesus late Friday afternoon. Having laid Him there, they rolled a disk-shaped stone into place over the entrance, ensuring that the tomb would remain sealed unless a handful of able men rolled the stone back up its track. A group of women watched these proceedings as they sat across the way. They marked the tomb's location and planned to return there after the Sabbath. Finally, shortly after Jesus' body was interred, the ruling priests placed guards at the tomb site and commanded them to defend the tomb against tampering. All of this indicates that the location of Jesus' tomb was known with pinpoint accuracy by dozens of people, and the mob of guards standing outside it practically advertised to all of Jerusalem that Jesus lay within.

The stage is now set for showing the incoherence of the "wrong tomb" theory. First, it assumes that the women who watched Jesus' burial forgot the tomb's location in a little more than 36 hours. This aspect of the "wrong tomb" argument may rely on a sexist viewpoint that regards women as less intelligent and reliable than men. Second, the theory does not explain why the women ran back to Jerusalem with reports not just of an empty tomb, but also of angelic visitors and a risen Jesus. Obviously, stumbling onto the wrong vacant tomb would not cause a normal person to see angels and a risen Jesus. Again, the theory requires that the women were incompetent and given to fits of mania, and that this served as the foundation for a movement that quickly won the allegiance of intelligent, competent people all over the world. Third, if the disciples (women first, men later) somehow managed to visit the wrong tomb and get hyped up about a resurrection, it's a safe bet that the disbelieving Jews would have quickly corrected their error by directing them to the right location. Thus the Christian movement would have died immediately. Fourth, given that the disciples did not expect Jesus to rise from the dead, and given the fact that they were initially skeptical about the women's resurrection report, the rest of the disciples would have double-checked to make sure that the women had not visited the wrong tomb. Certainly Joseph and Nicodemus would have gotten involved since they had interred the body. The mistake would have been corrected "in house" even before the disbelieving Jews had a chance to get involved. Fifth, this theory does not explain the repeated appearances of the risen Jesus to His disciples. The revolutionary Christian message was not just, "The tomb is empty," but rather, "Jesus is alive! We have seen and touched Him!" More than five hundred people made this claim in the days and weeks after Jesus' resurrection.

Women Witnesses—Some critics say the Gospel writers made up the story about Jesus' resurrection and then sold it as a true account in order to create a new religion and position themselves as its master priests. If the authors really had this much guile and cunning, we should find that they were careful to invent only elements, characters, and events that sounded credible to first-century readers. Make the story as believable as possible in order to increase the odds of winning a reader's assent. Conversely, they would not create elements that undermined believability. After all, a story that claims a man executed by state and religious officials came back to life after three days of entombment is already hard to believe. Adding other hard-to-swallow elements would only make it harder to believe. In this light, it is remarkable that the Gospel authors report that women were the first eyewitnesses of Jesus' resurrection. This put women at the epicenter of history's biggest moment. It is important to understand the social context of that era. Women were of low station in those times. They were uneducated, held few rights, and were not even permitted to testify in court because it was widely believed that they were too emotional to make sober assessments of important issues and events. Posting women at the resurrection scene would only undermine the credibility of the resurrection claim. Skeptical readers would note the reliance on women and say, "This is just a tale told by excitable women." In fact, Roman critics mocked Christianity for the prominence it gave to women; the Jews felt the same way. In this light we must ask why the Gospel authors would dare say that women were the first witnesses to the risen Jesus. The most sensible answer is that they were simply telling it like it was. These were honest men conveying an honest account of a true historical event. No doubt they were tempted to hide the women's involvement, but this impulse was overcome by an even greater desire to tell the truth. Women were the first to see Jesus alive, and the authors were unwilling to cover up this embarrassing but true fact.

Resurrection as Legend—Some critics claim that the original disciples never believed Jesus rose from the dead, but that over time a resurrection legend grew as people reminisced on a great man's life but lost sight of what really happened to Him. Key to this theory is the claim that full-blown resurrection belief did not arise until the eyewitnesses to Jesus' life had passed away, thus ensuring that no living person could correct and overturn the growing resurrection legend. Eventually the legend was incorporated into the written accounts of Jesus' life, the New Testament Gospels. Hence the Gospels reflect sincere but unfounded beliefs.

The first of several problems with this theory is that Jesus' original followers, especially the band of men who followed Him as His official students (they numbered 12 again after Judas was replaced) were at the very center of the Christian movement from its inception. They were among the first to see Jesus after He arose from the dead. After seeing Him over a period of 40 days following this, they watched Him ascend to heaven. They left this stunning scene and went to Jerusalem, where they gathered all of Jesus' followers and waited until God sent the Holy Spirit to officially form the church. This occurred barely more than a month after Jesus' execution. From that point forward the band of original disciples (called apostles now) were the official spokesmen for Christianity. In the years and decades that followed, their writings became the official documents of the Christian faith. These writings began to emerge as early as the late-40s, just a decade or so after Jesus' crucifixion. If Jesus' resurrection were merely a legend that developed in the late first and early second centuries, why do Christian writings dating from the mid-first century insist on the truth of His resurrection? This is an obvious and fatal flaw in the "resurrection as legend" theory. In fact, most likely all of the New Testament books were written within the lifetime of people who had been eyewitnesses to Jesus' life, death, and resurrection. This has at least one important implication: Had the New Testament books exaggerated the facts or invented unfounded stories about Jesus, especially the resurrection, these witnesses would have stood forward to stop the fabrications that were tainting the truth about their beloved Teacher. This is especially so since the resurrection teachings only earned the church mockery and persecution. Why allow a false teaching to stand if it only causes unwarranted trouble? The apostles would not have abided this. Therefore Jesus' resurrection is no mere legend. It is instead the most fantastic, hope-filled event in human history.

Resurrection as Late Invention—Have the Gospels been drastically altered since the day they were written? Some skeptics say so. They claim that the originals did not include the resurrection accounts or anything else that portrayed Jesus as God's divine Son. In its most cynical form this argument suggests power-hungry politicians and priests banded together and made a pact to recreate Christianity in an authoritarian, male-centric caste that runs counter to Jesus' original teachings. Those who altered Jesus' biography made Him into a divine Messiah because such a Messiah could better command the people's allegiance through an officially sanctioned priesthood. Authoritative documents (the New Testament writings) and authoritative magistrates (priests and politicians) could unite the people under a single banner and therefore exercise control over vast resources. Among the many flaws of this theory are the following: First, if the original writings are really lost to history, how can critics be sure that they did not contain the resurrection and other elements that teach Jesus' divinity? In other words, how can the critics prove that alterations have been made? *They cannot.* Second, all evidence points to a very early belief in the resurrection. Third, it takes a great deal of cynicism to suggest that a pack of greedy, unethical power brokers could invent a divine Jesus whose ethics are unmatched in all of history, whose teachings forbid leaders to seek personal fame or fortune, and whose self-giving sacrifice on the cross offers such indiscriminate hope to humanity. Fourth, though the early history of Christianity was of course dotted with a few unethical characters, the consistent testimony from that era proves that the early Christian leaders rejected the pursuit of worldly power in favor of a life devoted to Christ. The early Christian landscape is littered with Christians who embraced poverty, vowed chastity, and endured martyrdom for the sake of the gospel. Can these be the devotions of men who tricked the world into following a divine Jesus? Of course not. The "late invention" theory is deeply inadequate as an explanation for belief in Jesus' divinity and resurrection.

Reluctant Faith—Did Jesus' disciples jump on the bandwagon just as soon as someone came around talking resurrection? If so, we might have cause to suspect that they did not carefully weigh the evidence before deciding to believe in the resurrection. However, all evidence indicates that the disciples were reluctant to believe. When Mary Magdalene found Jesus' empty tomb, her first and only thought was that someone had played a cruel trick and stolen Jesus' body. Resurrection was not even in her vocabulary at that moment. She persisted in unbelief even after several of her companions saw the risen Jesus. In fact, she did not believe until she saw Jesus for herself. The same was true of Peter. He and John ran to the tomb and found it empty, just as Mary had said. John looked in and saw the empty facecloth that Joseph and Nicodemus had wrapped around His head before laying Him in the tomb. Seeing this strange wonder, John realized that Jesus had come alive and simply passed through the cloth. Not Peter. He was amazed at the sight, but amazement is not belief. He awaited greater evidence before he would believe that Jesus had come back to life. Then there is Thomas. *Doubting Thomas*, we call him. He was not present at the tomb or the first time Jesus appeared to the disciples in a closed room. Most likely he was off somewhere alone, trying to figure out what he would do with his life now that Jesus was dead. These were bitter days for Thomas. Had he wasted all those years following Jesus? A week after everyone else had seen Jesus, Thomas gathered with the rest of the disciples and told them that he would not join them in belief unless Jesus showed up and allowed him to poke around in His wounds. Here was a man who demanded strong evidence! Like all the other disciples, Thomas had never been able to accept that Messiah would die in the first place, let alone rise from the dead. It simply did not make sense to him. But then Jesus showed up and invited Thomas to probe His crucifixion wounds and settle all his doubts. Humbled, exhilarated, and overjoyed, Thomas put down his last defense and joined the ranks of those who accepted the truth of Jesus' resurrection.

Hype and Hallucination—Hope and expectation can be powerful forces. If you want a thing badly enough or if you fervently expect it to happen, you might just trick yourself into thinking it has in fact happened, especially if pressure and emotion combine in the right way. Did Jesus' followers fall into this sort of trap? Some critics see the resurrection story as evidence that the disciples "saw" the resurrected Jesus merely because that's what they wanted or expected to see. The classic expression of this theory says the disciples were united in hope that Jesus would come back to life and ended up sharing a mass hallucination of His resurrection. There are four fatal objections. First, Jesus' disciples did *not* expect Him to rise from the dead. The unanimous testimony of the Gospels is that the disciples could not comprehend Jesus' predictions that He would die and rise again, and a survey of Jewish literature from that era shows beyond doubt that *no one* expected Messiah to be executed and resurrected. Second, it is extremely doubtful that the sort of group hallucination on which this theory relies is even possible. After all, at one point after His resurrection Jesus appeared to a group of 500 people. On many other occasions he appeared to multiple persons. How could so many people share in an identical hallucination, especially a hallucination that ran counter to their expectations? Third, the consistent message of the apostles was that they and others had seen and *touched* the risen Jesus. In fact, Jesus even ate meals with them. No hallucination can explain this widespread claim. Fourth, the hallucination of a resurrected Jesus does not explain the reality of the empty tomb.

Did Jesus Die on the Cross?—Skeptics offer two arguments claiming that Jesus did not actually die on the cross. The *swoon* theory says Jesus was gravely injured but not killed during crucifixion. Mistaking Him for dead, the soldiers hauled an unconscious Jesus down from the cross and handed Him into the care of Joseph, who then wrapped and entombed the body. After several days of lying in the cool, quiet tomb, Jesus felt revived enough to get up and show Himself to His followers. There are several outstanding problems with this theory. First, a revived but wounded Jesus would not be able unravel the grave wrappings that pinned His arms snug against his body and bound His legs together. Besides that, He would not be able to roll away the tomb's sealing stone and exit. He would be alive but trapped in the dark. Finally, even if Jesus somehow made his way out of the tomb, his wounds would have required immediate medical attention. It is inconceivable that His followers would think He had conquered death if in fact He was dragging around half dead. The other theory denying that Jesus died on the cross is called the *replacement* theory. It says that due to a colossal mix-up or a deft maneuver, someone else was executed in Jesus' place. Hence, the crowds thought Jesus had been killed when in reality He was alive and well. This is an extremely unlikely scenario because it supposes that the soldiers, priests, and bystanders were all fooled. It also fails to explain how the resurrection story arose in the first place. If Jesus had never been nailed to the cross, His movement would have hailed Him as an elusive and crafty Messiah, not a resurrected Messiah.

The Verdict of Science—Science indicates that genuinely dead bodies do not come back to life by natural means, but it cannot demonstrate that such a thing is impossible by *super*natural means. By definition miracles are performed by a supernatural force that cannot be encompassed or examined by scientists and their tools, all of which are confined to the natural world. Ironically, science's restriction against the resurrection of a mutilated, three-days-dead body actually highlights the reality of God's involvement in Jesus' return from death. After all, there is no way that Jesus could suffer 40 lashes, nail punctures at His wrists and ankles, and a deep stab into the chest, and yet come bounding back to life after being stuffed cocoon-like into a sealed tomb. Science affirms what faith accepts: Jesus' return from death was a miracle.

Lifestyle and Message—When Jesus was arrested and crucified, His disciples panicked, fled, and sank into despondency. Days later they joyously embarked on a lifelong mission to spread faith in the risen Jesus. In city after city, country after country, Christ's followers renounced worldly pursuits and preached that Jesus is God's Son, that He died for our sins, and that on the third day He arose. Importantly, this message got them in trouble everywhere they went. They were mocked, beaten, imprisoned, and eventually killed because they would not shut up about Jesus and His triumph over death. Jews labeled them as blasphemers and Greeks thought they were fools. If the disciples knew or even suspected that the resurrection was false, they would have given up Christianity and gone on with their lives, earning better money and reputation as they enfolded themselves back into the mainstream. They never did this because they knew beyond all doubt that Jesus really did rise from the dead.

Explosive Growth—The explosive growth of a religious movement whose leader was condemned and executed as a scoundrel, blasphemer, and disrupter of the peace is difficult to explain unless, as Christianity says, the leader was vindicated by resurrection. The earliest believers forsook everything to spread the radical, life-giving message about Jesus' death for us and His return to life. Their devotion to this message is especially amazing when you consider that no one expected Messiah to suffer and die, let alone emerge from a tomb. According to the book of Acts, the church grew because of God's powerful presence. Miracles and works of power were performed by the apostles as God vouched for the message they were preaching.

Conclusion—All attempts to refute Jesus' resurrection are less plausible than the resurrection itself. Unless one is biased against belief in God or miracles, the data indicates that Jesus is alive today. This is the greatest story of hope that has ever been told, and it happens to be *true*. Jesus is alive and He invites you to follow Him and gain pardon from sins and eternal life in heaven. How faith in Jesus' life, death, and resurrection can bring such fantastic benefits is explained below.

What the Cross Means to You

The cross was a scene of indescribable horror for Jesus, but not chiefly for the reasons you may think. Certainly the piercing nails, torn flesh, and taunting crowds pained Him, but His greatest suffering was due to an invisible transaction in which God the Father poured out His wrath against human sin. Earth shook and the sky blackened as God punished His innocent Son for the wrongdoings of humanity. Why did it happen this way? What does Jesus' suffering and death mean for you and me? To find answers, we must first identify the human condition.

The Bible teaches that God made humans in His image. This means we are rational, personal beings who think, relate, and make choices that shape the world. The Bible also says all humans have broken union with God by choosing sin over righteousness. This means we are all rebels and law-breakers. The moral laws that we have broken are not merely items on God's list of do's and don'ts; rather, the laws reflect God's eternal nature. God is holiness itself. His laws serve as guidelines for defining His holiness and His expectations for our lifestyles. Any *un*holy act or disposition is therefore *anti*-God. Sin is not just a bending of rules, therefore, but an assault on God's being. This means you personally are guilty of aggressions against your Maker. The moral fabric of the universe would tear to pieces if God were to let such rebellion go unpunished, for this would mean that His character, nature, and laws do not matter. God will not allow this, and so humans need atonement for sins. To *atone* means to make right on a broken relationship or to repair a wrong. The terms or stipulations for atonement must be defined by God, not humans, for it is God who is offended.

What does God require for atonement? In the Old Testament He revealed that animal sacrifices should be made. The lifeblood of sinless bulls and goats was spilled over Hebrew altars in expression of sinful humanity's need for pardon from God, but this was merely a provisional method since the blood of animals cannot serve as an adequate replacement for the errant humans to whom God's wrath is due. To serve as an adequate substitute in God's atonement program, the sacrificial victim needs to be sinless, truly representative of humanity, and able to bear on His lone moral frame the debt owed by countless sinners. Obviously this means we are describing the need for a human sacrifice. More to the point: a *superhuman* sacrifice. This is the most breathtaking reality of the Bible. The holy God who made humans in His image would someday require that one of His image bearers, a morally perfect human being, stand in the place of His fellows and give satisfaction for the boundless sin debt. What man could be adequate for such a task? Only one: Jesus the divine Messiah, sent from heaven to be a human and a stand-in for Adam's stray children.

Jesus lived as the ideal human. He loved God above all else, obeyed Him always, and loved His neighbors as Himself. This made Jesus the ideal substitute for God's requirement that a man acceptable to Him should live in complete righteousness from beginning to end. Due to this perfect righteousness and His divine capacities to endure the Father's infinite wrath against sins, Jesus presented Himself as the only sufficient substitute for our death penalty. Therefore on the cross Jesus endured not just the punishment that men handed out but also *God's in-*

finite punishment against sin as the divine holy nature struck the curse Jesus had become. Jesus *became sin* so that God could judge sin in human flesh and thereby satisfy the requirements of His justice. By faith in Christ's death and resurrection you and I can enjoy full pardon from God not because God just let us off the hook but because Jesus fully satisfied God's wrath by enduring the blows that were due us. We can live because He died in our place.

Christianity and Truth

Christianity is false if Jesus did not rise from the dead. Believers and skeptics alike recognize this, and so for centuries people have examined Christian foundations in an attempt to judge their dependability. In modern times one of the most widely publicized quests for truth was conducted by a journalist named Lee Strobel. As he explains below, a careful examination of the evidences can lead to a surprising result.

How Apologetics Changed My Life

By Lee Strobel
Author, *The Case for Christ*

Skepticism is in my DNA. That's why I combined the study of law and journalism to become the legal editor of *The Chicago Tribune*—a career in which I relentlessly pursued hard facts. That's also why I was attracted to a thorough examination of the evidence as a way to probe the legitimacy of Christianity. As a spiritual cynic, I became an atheist in high school. To me the concept of an all-loving, all-knowing, all-powerful Creator was absurd and didn't warrant consideration. I believed that God didn't create people, but that people created God out of fear of death and a desire to live forever in a utopia (heaven). Fittingly, I married an agnostic named Leslie. Several years later she came to me with the worst news possible: she had decided to follow Jesus. My initial thought was that she was going to turn into an irrational holy roller who would waste all of her time serving the poor in a soup kitchen. Divorce, I figured, was inevitable.

Then something amazing occurred. I saw positive changes in Leslie's character, values, and the way she related to me and the kids. The transformation was winsome and attractive, and so when she invited me to church one day, I complied. The pastor spelled out the essentials in a talk called "Basic Christianity." He didn't convert me that day, but I knew that if he was speaking truth, it would have huge implications. That's when I decided to apply my experience as a journalist to investigating whether there is any credibility to Christianity or other faith systems. I resolved to keep an open mind and follow the evidence—even if it took me to uncomfortable conclusions.

I thought my investigation would be short-lived. In my opinion, having "faith" meant you believed something you knew couldn't be true. I anticipated that I would uncover facts that would devastate Christianity. Yet as I devoured books by atheists and Christians, interviewed scientists and theologians, and studied archaeology, ancient history, and world religions, I was stunned to find that Christianity's factual foundation was a lot firmer than I had believed.

Much of my investigation focused on science, where recent discoveries have only further cemented the conclusions I drew in those studies. For instance, cosmologists say that the universe and time itself came into existence in the finite past. The logic is inexorable: whatever begins to exist has a cause, the universe began to exist, and therefore the universe has a cause.

It makes sense that this cause must be immaterial, timeless, powerful, and intelligent. What's more, physicists have discovered that many of the laws and constants of the universe are finely tuned to an incomprehensible precision in order for life to exist. This exactitude defies the explanation of mere chance.

The information in DNA also points toward a Creator. Each of our cells contains assembly instructions for every protein out of which our bodies are made, all spelled out in a four-letter chemical alphabet. Nature can produce patterns, but whenever we see *information*, we know intelligence lies behind it. Furthermore, there are complex biological machines on the cellular level that defy a Darwinian explanation. They can only be explained as the work of an Intelligent Designer.

To my astonishment, I became convinced *by the evidence* that science supports belief in a Creator who looks suspiciously like the God of the Bible. Spurred on by my discoveries, I turned my attention to history. There I found that Jesus fulfilled ancient messianic prophecies against all odds. I concluded that the New Testament is rooted in eyewitness testimony and that it passes the tests that historians use to determine reliability. I learned that the Bible has been passed down through the ages with remarkable fidelity. However, the pivotal issue for me was the resurrection of Jesus. Anyone can claim to be the Son of God, as Jesus clearly did. The question was whether Jesus could back up that assertion by miraculously returning from the dead. One by one, the facts built a convincing and compelling case. Jesus' death by crucifixion is as certain as anything in the ancient world. The accounts of His resurrection are too early to be the product of legendary developme nt. Even the enemies of Jesus conceded that His tomb was empty on Easter morning. And the eyewitness encounters with the risen Jesus cannot be explained away as mere hallucinations or wishful thinking.

This just scratches the surface of what I uncovered in my nearly two-year investigation. Frankly, I was completely surprised by the depth and breadth of the case for Christianity. As someone trained in journalism and law, I felt I had no choice but to respond to the facts. So on November 8, 1981, I took a step of faith in the same direction that the evidence was pointing and became a follower of Jesus. And just like my wife, over time my character, values, and priorities began to change for the good.

For me, apologetics (the examination and defense of Christian belief) was the turning point of my life and eternity. I'm thankful for the scholars who defend the truth of Christianity, and now my life's goal is to help others get answers to the questions that are blocking their spiritual journey toward Christ.

Your Search for Answers

Lee Strobel disbelieved Christianity until he examined the evidence with a critical but open mind. What about you? Have you looked at the evidence? The Gospels are a great place to start. In the remainder of this book you will find the Gospel of John, including the footnotes and essays that appear in the *Apologetics Study Bible* (www.ApologeticsBible.com), a study aid in which world-class scholars provide answers to tough questions about Christianity. For instance, Gary Habermas probes Jesus' teachings to test whether they are unique. He also writes an essay that speaks forthrightly about doubt. J. P. Moreland and Hank Hanegraaff present evidence for life after death, and New Testament scholar Craig Blomberg provides penetrating notes on apologetics issues in John. If you are willing to follow Strobel's bold example of truth-seeking, examine the Gospel of John for yourself.

JOHN

AUTHOR

*D*espite doubts from various quarters, a good case can be made that the fourth Gospel was written by John, the "one Jesus loved" (as he referred to himself throughout his book), brother of James and son of Zebedee, just as early church tradition suggests. That same tradition places John in and around Ephesus, ministering to the churches of Asia Minor, until his death as an elderly man at roughly the end of the first century. The author would thus have been an eyewitness of much of the material he recounted and in a position to provide accurate information. The Gospel appears to be the first of five books he wrote in the A.D. 90s, the next ones being the three NT letters that bear his name and the book of Revelation.

It is possible that John relied on earlier written sources for some of the information in his Gospel, especially for the miracles of Jesus, where a different style and vocabulary at times intrude. In particular, it is possible that he knew one or more of the first three (Synoptic) Gospels. John's Gospel seems to be literarily independent of them, however. More likely he was aware of their contents more from oral tradition and an active preaching ministry and wanted to supplement them by focusing on different information in his account.

Without question, John's writing style, like his selection of content and themes, differs noticeably from that of the Synoptics. As was perfectly acceptable in his day, he would have written his account of what others said in his own distinctive style, being faithful to their meaning if not to their exact wording. His sense of being led by the Holy Spirit (14:26; 15:26; 16:13) would have given him the freedom to couch things in his own words, believing he was being faithful to history at the same time.

THEMES

A list of themes that receive distinctive emphasis in John, as compared with the Synoptics, includes a strong belief in the full deity of Jesus as well as His full humanity, an emphasis on the availability of eternal life to all who believe in Jesus (beginning already in this life), miracles as signs meant to elicit faith in Christ, the beginnings of Trinitarian thought, the unity of disciples, the election and security of the believer, the death of Christ as exaltation and glorification, the Holy Spirit as Comforter (Counselor, Advocate), a playing down of the role of John the Baptist and of the baptism and the Lord's Supper and a strong polemic against unbelieving Judaism.

Many of these themes can be explained by the situation in which John's churches found themselves. The minority of believers from Jewish backgrounds by this time were largely ostracized by the local synagogues and may have begun to wonder if they had made the right choice in following Jesus. John's Gospel provided them with much "ammunition" in their quest to evangelize their non-Christian Jewish friends and family and encouraged them in the belief that Jesus is the true fulfillment of all of the central hopes and aspirations of Judaism. Ephesus, however, was also being infiltrated by the early Gnostic teacher Cerinthus, who taught a form of docetism—the belief that Christ only "seemed" (from the Gk *dokeo*) to be human. Hence, John emphasized Jesus' full deity and His full humanity.

DIFFERENCES BETWEEN JOHN'S GOSPEL AND THE SYNOPTICS

*T*he apologist will probably be most interested in the numerous differences between John and the Synoptics and how they can be explained in detail. John includes no parables, few kingdom teachings, no exorcisms, and no pronouncement stories (short debates with hostile questioners ending in climactic pronouncements). But the parable seems to have been a distinctively Jewish form of teaching not known to the Greeks. The kingdom was an OT theocratic concept that likewise could have misled a largely Gentile church. Exorcisms were viewed almost magically in the Greco-Roman world, and John does include plenty of more extended controversies with Jewish leaders.

More telling are examples of "interlocking" between John and the Synoptics—places where details in one Gospel help explain what might have remained mysterious in another. For example, John refers to the imprisonment of John the Baptist ever so briefly (Jn 3:24), but only the Synoptics narrate the actual story (Mk 6:14-29). John 11:2 distinguishes Mary the sister of Lazarus from Mary the mother of Jesus by alluding to a story John has not yet narrated but that Mark said would be recounted whenever the gospel is preached (Mk 14:9). And the references to Jesus' trial before Caiaphas (Jn 18:24,28) are so short as to presuppose the fuller detail known from the first three Gospels (Mk 14:53-65).

In other instances John clarifies something the Synoptics leave puzzling. Why did the garbled charges against Jesus at His trial claim that He had predicted He would destroy the temple (Mk 14:58-59)? Presumably, because of what He said two years earlier about destroying the temple, when His audience didn't understand He was talking about His own body (Jn 2:19). Why did the Jewish Sanhedrin involve the Roman authorities with Jesus' execution in the first place, since their law prescribed stoning for blasphemy (Mk 15:1-3)? Most probably, it was because Rome prevented the Jews from carrying out capital punishment in most instances (Jn 18:31). How could the Synoptics describe Jesus as often wanting to gather the children of Jerusalem together (Mt 23:37) when they narrate only one trip the adult Jesus took to the holy city—that of His final Passover? Doubtless because He did in fact go there regularly at festival times, as John repeatedly indicates (chaps. 2; 5; 7–9; 10). Indeed, it is only from John that we learn that Jesus' ministry lasted for roughly three years, a claim most scholars accept as accurate. Plenty of additional examples of interlocking in each direction could be given.

A key feature of John's literary genre provides further explanation of the book's distinctives. John was less literal in his reporting than the authors of the Synoptics, in large measure due to writing in a style somewhat akin to ancient Greco-Roman drama. But his recurring emphasis on themes like truth and witness shows that he believed he was faithfully reproducing the life and times of Jesus even through this genre.

A detailed analysis of the historical reliability of John proceeds through the Gospel, verse by verse, looking for compatibility with the Synoptic data and applying standard historical criteria for authenticity to each text in turn. The most helpful criterion is what has been called *double similarity and dissimilarity*. When a teaching or event from Jesus' life fits plausibly into the Jewish world of Israel during the first third of the first century but differs in some respect from most conventional Judaism of the day, it is not likely to have been invented by some Jew other than Jesus. When that same teaching or event also shows some continuity with later Christian belief or practice and yet likewise proves distinctive at some telling point, it is not likely to have been manufactured by any later Christian. Usually at least one central element, if not several, emerge in each passage in John to satisfy this four-part criterion.

Much scholarship today continues to dismiss John as not nearly as valuable for recovering the "historical Jesus" as the Synoptics, but this scholarship rarely interacts in detail with the studies that demonstrate the points briefly summarized in this introduction.

None of this suggests that historical research can "prove" the reliability of every last detail in John (or any other portion of Scripture). But when writers prove repeatedly reliable where they can be tested, they should be given the benefit of the doubt where they cannot be checked. Christian belief in the full trustworthiness, authority, and inspiration or inerrancy of the text requires a leap of faith beyond what historical evidence alone can demonstrate. But it is not a leap in the dark, flying in the face of the evidence. It is a conscious choice consistent with the evidence that does exist.

Prologue

1 In the beginning was the Word,[a]
and the Word was with God,
and the Word was God.

[2] He was with God in the beginning.

[3] All things were created through Him,
and apart from Him not one thing
was created
that has been created.

[4] Life was in Him,[b]
and that life was the light of men.

[5] That light shines in the darkness,
yet the darkness did not overcome[c] it.

[6] There was a man named John
who was sent from God.

[7] He came as a witness
to testify about the light,
so that all might believe through him.[d]

[8] He was not the light,
but he came to testify about the light.

[9] The true light, who gives light
to everyone,
was coming into the world.[e]

[10] He was in the world,
and the world was created through Him,
yet the world did not recognize Him.

[11] He came to His own,[f]
and His own people[f]
did not receive Him.

[12] But to all who did receive Him,
He gave them the right to be[g]
children of God,
to those who believe in His name,

[13] who were born,
not of blood,[h]
or of the will of the flesh,
or of the will of man,[i]
but of God.

[14] The Word became flesh[j]
and took up residence[k] among us.
We observed His glory,
the glory as the One and Only Son[l]
from the Father,

TWISTED SCRIPTURE
John 1:1-2,14

These verses refute Unitarian and cultic efforts to strip Jesus of His deity. They also hint at a Trinity. As the Word, Jesus "was God" (v. 1) and was "with God" (v. 2), indicating that the eternal Godhead consists of more than one person. The Word was incarnated as a human and dwelt among us (v. 14).

[a]1:1 The *Word* (Gk *Logos*) is a title for Jesus as the communication and the revealer of God the Father; Jn 1:14,18; Rv 19:13. [b]1:3–4 Other punctuation is possible: . . . *not one thing was created. What was created in Him was life* [c]1:5 Or *grasp*, or *comprehend*, or *overtake*; Jn 12:35 [d]1:7 Or *through it* (the light) [e]1:9 Or *The true light who comes into the world gives light to everyone*, or *The true light enlightens everyone coming into the world.* [f]1:11 The same Gk adjective is used twice in this verse: the first refers to all that Jesus owned as Creator (*to His own*); the second refers to the Jews (*His own people*). [g]1:12 Or *become* [h]1:13 Lit *bloods*; the pl form of *blood* occurs only here in the NT. It may refer either to lineal descent (that is, blood from one's father and mother) or to the OT sacrificial system (that is, the various blood sacrifices). Neither is the basis for birth into the family of God. [i]1:13 Or *not of human lineage, or of human capacity, or of human volition* [j]1:14 The eternally existent Word (vv. 1–2) took on full humanity, but without sin; Heb 4:15. [k]1:14 Lit *and tabernacled, or and dwelt in a tent*; this word occurs only here in John. A related word, referring to the Festival of Tabernacles, occurs only in 7:2; Ex 40:34–38. [l]1:14 *Son* is implied from the reference to the Father and from Gk usage.

1:1 There is no definite article ("the") in the Greek before "God," so the Jehovah's Witnesses' New World Translation reads, "The Word was a god." But sentences of this form in Greek (two nouns joined by a form of the verb "to be") normally placed the article only before the subject of the sentence, regardless of word order. So the traditional translation, "The Word was God," is to be preferred.

1:4,7,9 Each of these three verses could suggest that all people will be saved. But verses 5, 10, and 11 all make it clear that not everyone accepted Jesus. So John must have meant that salvation was available through Jesus for all people, not that salvation automatically is applied to all people.

1:11 "He came to His own" probably referred first of all to the Jews. But if the Jews rejected the one claiming to be their Messiah, why should anyone else believe in Him? We must remember that throughout the OT period the majority of the Jewish people, more often than not, rebelled against God. But there was always a righteous remnant, as there was in the days of Jesus and the apostles. The number of people who believe something is not always related to the truth of what is believed.

1:14 Ancient Gnostics and modern "New Agers" have often challenged the idea of God taking on human flesh, since "flesh" is seen as inherently corrupt. But Gn 1 stresses that God created the world and everything in it to be completely good. Only later did sin corrupt everything. Jesus, however, was God's "new creation" and free from sin. God Himself became incarnate in order to redeem sinful humanity.

full of grace and truth.

¹⁵ (John testified concerning Him
and exclaimed,

"This was the One of whom
I said,

'The One coming after me
has surpassed me,
because He existed before me.'")

¹⁶ Indeed, we have all received grace
after grace

from His fullness,

¹⁷ for although the law was given
through Moses,
grace and truth came
through Jesus Christ.

¹⁸ No one has ever seen God.ᵃ
The One and Only Sonᵇ—
the One who is
at the Father's sideᶜ—
He has revealed Him.

ᵃ1:18 Since God is an infinite being, no one can see Him in His absolute essential nature; Ex 33:18–23.   ᵇ1:18 Other mss read *God*   ᶜ1:18 Lit *is in the bosom of the Father*

1:17 This verse could suggest a complete dichotomy between OT and NT times, but in the context of verse 16 it must refer to a relative contrast. A literal translation from the Greek of verse 16 says (NT) grace "instead of" (OT) grace. Grace appears throughout the OT. God's deliverance of Israel from Egypt was an act of grace. Comparatively, however, the NT focuses on grace even more because it describes the completed plan of salvation in Christ.

1:18 If no one has ever seen God the Father, how could the Lord appear to OT saints, wrestle with Jacob, show His back to Moses, etc.? Because "God is spirit" (4:24) and because a spirit "does not have flesh and bones" (Lk 24:39), God is not inherently embodied. But He appeared to people temporarily in bodily form in OT times as a precursor to His full incarnation in Jesus.

Aren't the Gospels the Product of Greek Thinking?

by Ronald H. Nash

For more than a century, liberal critics of the Christian faith have been claiming that early Christianity was heavily influenced by Platonism, Stoicism, pagan mystery religions, or other movements in the world at that time. A series of scholarly books and articles had refuted most of these claims by the 1940s. But new generations of liberal scholars have revived many of these older discredited positions.

The favorite target among the four Gospels has been the Gospel of John. John 1:1-18 was supposedly influenced by a Jewish philosopher named Philo who lived in Alexandria, Egypt. Rudolf Bultmann made a career of claiming that parts of John's Gospel were influenced by Gnosticism and/or various mystery religions. Such influences allegedly extended to the Apostle Paul as well.

All Christians should ask the following questions of all claims about any alleged dependence of early Christianity upon pagan sources:

(1) What is the evidence for such claims?

(2) What are the dates for the evidence? An embarrassingly high percentage of the alleged evidence turns out to be dated long after the writing of the NT.

(3) Are the alleged parallels really similar, or are the likenesses a result of exaggeration, oversimplification, inattention to detail, or the use of Christian language in the description?

(4) Is the alleged parallel between the NT and a supposed pagan source the sort of thing that could have arisen independently in several different movements?

(5) Is the claim of influence or dependence consistent with the historical information we have about the first-century church?

ARTICLE

John the Baptist's Testimony

[19] This is John's testimony when the Jews from Jerusalem sent priests and Levites to ask him, "Who are you?"

[20] He did not refuse to answer, but he declared: "I am not the Messiah."

[21] "What then?" they asked him. "Are you Elijah?"

"I am not," he said.

"Are you the Prophet?"[a]

"No," he answered.

[22] "Who are you, then?" they asked. "We need to give an answer to those who sent us. What can you tell us about yourself?"

[23] He said, "I am a **voice of one crying out in the wilderness: Make straight the way of the Lord**[b]—just as Isaiah the prophet said."

[24] Now they had been sent from the Pharisees. [25] So they asked him, "Why then do you baptize if you aren't the Messiah, or Elijah, or the Prophet?"

[26] "I baptize with[c] water," John answered them. "Someone stands among you, but you don't know ⌊Him⌋. [27] He is the One coming after me,[d] whose sandal strap I'm not worthy to untie."

[28] All this happened in Bethany[e] across the Jordan,[f] where John was baptizing.

The Lamb of God

[29] The next day John saw Jesus coming toward him and said, "Here is the Lamb of God, who takes away the sin of the world! [30] This is the One I told you about: 'After me comes a man who has surpassed me, because He existed before me.' [31] I didn't know Him, but I came baptizing with[c] water so He might be revealed to Israel."

[32] And John testified, "I watched the Spirit descending from heaven like a dove, and He rested on Him. [33] I didn't know Him, but He[g] who sent me to baptize with[c] water told me, 'The One you see the Spirit descending and resting on—He is the One who baptizes with[c] the Holy Spirit.' [34] I have seen and testified that He is the Son of God!"[h]

[35] Again the next day, John was standing with two of his disciples. [36] When he saw Jesus passing by, he said, "Look! The Lamb of God!"

[37] The two disciples heard him say this and followed Jesus. [38] When Jesus turned and noticed them following Him, He asked them, "What are you looking for?"

They said to Him, "Rabbi" (which means "Teacher"), "where are You staying?"

[39] "Come and you'll see," He replied. So they went and saw where He was staying, and they stayed with Him that day. It was about 10 in the morning.[i]

a1:21 Probably = the Prophet in Dt 18:15 b1:23 Is 40:3 c1:26,31,33 Or *in* d1:27 Other mss add *who came before me* e1:28 Other mss read *in Bethabara* f1:28 Another Bethany, near Jerusalem, was the home of Lazarus, Martha, and Mary; Jn 11:1. g1:33 *He* refers to God the Father, who gave John a sign to help him identify the Messiah. Vv. 32–34 indicate that John did not know that Jesus was the Messiah until the Spirit descended upon Him at His baptism. h1:34 Other mss read *is the Chosen One of God* i1:39 Lit *about the tenth hour.* Various methods of reckoning time were used in the ancient world. John probably used a different method from the other 3 Gospels. If John used the same method of time reckoning as the other 3 Gospels, the translation would be: *It was about four in the afternoon.*

1:21 How could John deny that he was Elijah, when Jesus called him precisely that in Mt 11:14? Presumably he was denying that he was the literal Elijah returned from heaven that some Jews looked for. Luke 1:17 harmonizes the two texts: John came "in the spirit and power of Elijah."

1:28 The only Bethany we know of was close to Jerusalem, not "across" the Jordan River (to the east). This doesn't mean that John made a mistake, but it highlights our incomplete understanding of the archaeological history of the region. For example, there is a place called Batanea farther to the north, and east of Galilee, which may have been the place John called Bethany.

1:31 How could John have not previously known Jesus, since they were relatives and each had had a special

birth (see Lk 1–2)? John must have meant that after years had gone by and Jesus had done nothing extraordinary as a youth, he was not at all sure what the various prophecies about Jesus meant, until God further revealed things to him at Jesus' baptism.

1:36,41,45,49 In a short span of time Jesus was called the "Lamb of God," "Messiah," the "One Moses wrote about," the "Son of God," and the "King of Israel." How could Jesus' first followers know so much about Him so quickly, especially when the other Gospels do not include such understanding until much later in His ministry? Actually, all these titles carried with them the common Jewish expectation of a kingly, militaristic deliverer who would overthrow Rome. A full understanding of who Jesus was came slowly.

⁴⁰ Andrew, Simon Peter's brother, was one of the two who heard John and followed Him. ⁴¹ He first found his own brother Simon and told him, "We have found the Messiah!"ᵃ (which means "Anointed One"), ⁴² and he brought ⌊Simon⌋ to Jesus.

When Jesus saw him, He said, "You are Simon, son of John.ᵇ You will be called Cephas" (which means "Rock").

Philip and Nathanael

⁴³ The next day Heᶜ decided to leave for Galilee. Jesus found Philip and told him, "Follow Me!"

⁴⁴ Now Philip was from Bethsaida, the hometown of Andrew and Peter. ⁴⁵ Philip found Nathanaelᵈ and told him, "We have found the One Moses wrote about in the Law (and so did the prophets): Jesus the son of Joseph, from Nazareth!"

⁴⁶ "Can anything good come out of Nazareth?" Nathanael asked him.

"Come and see," Philip answered.

⁴⁷ Then Jesus saw Nathanael coming toward Him and said about him, "Here is a true Israelite; no deceit is in him."

⁴⁸ "How do you know me?" Nathanael asked.

"Before Philip called you, when you were under the fig tree, I saw you," Jesus answered.

⁴⁹ "Rabbi," Nathanael replied, "You are the Son of God! You are the King of Israel!"

⁵⁰ Jesus responded to him, "Do you believe ⌊only⌋ because I told you I saw you under the fig tree? Youᵉ will see greater things than this." ⁵¹ Then He said, "I assure you: Youᶠ will see heaven opened and the angels of God ascending and descending on the Son of Man."

The First Sign: Turning Water into Wine

On the third day a wedding took place in Cana of Galilee. Jesus' mother was there, and ² Jesus and His disciples were invited to the wedding as well. ³ When the wine ran out, Jesus' mother told Him, "They don't have any wine."

⁴ "What has this concern of yours to do with Me,ᵍ woman?" Jesus asked. "My hourʰ has not yet come."

⁵ "Do whatever He tells you," His mother told the servants.

⁶ Now six stone water jars had been set there for Jewish purification. Each contained 20 or 30 gallons.ⁱ

ᵃ1:41 In the NT, the word Messiah translates the Gk word *Christos* ("Anointed One"), except here and in Jn 4:25 where it translates *Messias*. ᵇ1:42 Other mss read *Simon, son of Jonah* ᶜ1:43 Or *he*, referring either to Peter (v. 42) or Andrew (vv. 40–41) ᵈ1:45 Probably the Bartholomew of the other Gospels and Acts ᵉ1:50 *You* (sg in Gk) refers to Nathanael. ᶠ1:51 *You* is pl in Gk and refers to Nathanael and the other disciples. ᵍ2:4 Or *You and I see things differently*; lit *What to Me and to you*; Mt 8:29; Mk 1:24; 5:7; Lk 8:28 ʰ2:4 The time of His sacrificial death and exaltation; Jn 7:30; 8:20; 12:23,27; 13:1; 17:1 ⁱ2:6 Lit *2 or 3 measures*

1:42 Doesn't this verse contradict Mt 16:18, in which Jesus much later called Simon "the Rock" (Kepha [Cephas] in Aramaic and Petros [Peter] in Greek)? No, because in this verse Jesus used the future tense "will be called" and in the event at Caesarea Philippi He simply said, "You are . . ."

1:45 Jesus' being called "son of Joseph" does not contradict the traditions of a virginal conception. Joseph would have legally adopted Jesus and become His stepfather. Nathanael is probably the same person as Bartholomew (Mk 3:18).

1:46 It is sometimes claimed that we have no evidence of Nazareth existing as a town in Jesus' day. Yet artifacts show evidence of a settlement even before Roman times, as well as during the early Roman period, while a first-century inscription contains the name of Nazareth in Hebrew. But Nazareth was a small, out-of-the-way place that no one later wanting to honor Jesus would likely have made up. It is mentioned because that is where He really lived.

1:51 John's language sounds confused. We might expect angels coming and going from heaven to "descend and ascend," not the reverse. But John was alluding to Gn 28:12, in which Jacob dreamed about a stairway on which angels were "going up and down." Heaven will again open at Christ's resurrection and at His return; angels will accompany Him to heaven and one day usher Him back to earth.

2:4 Jesus' literal words to Mary sound brusque: "What has this concern of yours to do with Me, woman?" But another translation would be "Dear woman, why do you involve me?" It was not yet His time to provide for all the needs of all the world's people through His sacrificial death, but His turning water into wine was a sign that the messianic times had arrived (see Jl 3:13; Am 9:13-14).

2:6-7 Creating this much wine would seem to encourage drunkenness. Worse, this miracle seems to be frivolous from start to finish, hardly meeting any acute human need. On the other hand, wedding festivities often

[7] "Fill the jars with water," Jesus told them. So they filled them to the brim. [8] Then He said to them, "Now draw some out and take it to the chief servant."[a] And they did.

[9] When the chief servant tasted the water (after it had become wine), he did not know where it came from—though the servants who had drawn the water knew. He called the groom [10] and told him, "Everybody sets out the fine wine first, then, after people have drunk freely, the inferior. But you have kept the fine wine until now."

[11] Jesus performed this first sign[b] in Cana of Galilee. He displayed His glory, and His disciples believed in Him.

[12] After this, He went down to Capernaum, together with His mother, His brothers, and His disciples, and they stayed there only a few days.

Cleansing the Temple Complex

[13] The Jewish Passover was near, so Jesus went up to Jerusalem. [14] In the temple complex He found people selling oxen, sheep, and doves, and ⌊He also found⌋ the money changers sitting there. [15] After making a whip out of cords, He drove everyone out of the temple complex with their sheep and oxen. He also poured out the money changers' coins and overturned the tables. [16] He told those who were selling doves, "Get these things out of here! Stop turning My Father's house into a marketplace!"[c]

[17] And His disciples remembered that it is written: **Zeal for Your house will consume Me.**[d]

[18] So the Jews replied to Him, "What sign ⌊of authority⌋ will You show us for doing these things?"

[19] Jesus answered, "Destroy this sanctuary, and I will raise it up in three days."

[20] Therefore the Jews said, "This sanctuary took 46 years to build, and will You raise it up in three days?"

[21] But He was speaking about the sanctuary of His body. [22] So when He was raised from the dead, His disciples remembered that He had said this. And they believed the Scripture and the statement Jesus had made.

[23] While He was in Jerusalem at the Passover Festival, many trusted in His name when they saw the signs He was doing. [24] Jesus, however, would not entrust Himself to them, since He knew them all [25] and because He did not need anyone to testify about man; for He Himself knew what was in man.

Jesus and Nicodemus

3 There was a man from the Pharisees named Nicodemus, a ruler of the Jews. [2] This man came to Him at night and said, "Rabbi, we know that You have come

---

[a]2:8 Lit *ruler of the table*; perhaps *master of the feast*, or *headwaiter*   [b]2:11 Lit *this beginning of the signs*; Jn 4:54; 20:30. Seven miraculous signs occur in John's Gospel and are so noted in the headings.   [c]2:16 Lit *a house of business*   [d]2:17 Ps 69:9

---

lasted for a week and an entire village could have been involved, so the amounts consumed by any individual at one time may have been quite moderate. Furthermore, one of the points of the miracle was to stress the new joy associated with Jesus' ministry and the kingdom He was inaugurating. Mark 2:21-22 makes much the same point in the parable of the wineskins.

2:13-25 At first glance this passage seems out of place since the other Gospels all have Jesus clearing the temple during the last week of His life (Mk 11:15-17). But John may have thematically relocated this passage as a kind of "headline" over his entire Gospel (there are no precise chronological links with previous or subsequent material in the Greek), or Jesus may have cleared the temple twice—once at the outset of His ministry when He had the people's sympathies and once later when it proved too much for the authorities to tolerate.

2:15-16 Doesn't Jesus' "temple tantrum" show a cruel, vindictive side to Him—abusing animals and exhibiting uncontrollable rage? Actually, the Greek text says He applied the whip only to the wicked people He was confronting. Rabbinic sources suggest that using the temple for trading in sacrificial animals was a recent development; the Kidron Valley below had been the earlier site. Commercial convenience created the change, but it prevented the Court of the Gentiles from being used as God had intended it—as a place of worship. Godly wrath is eternal opposition to what is evil. As such, it is not at all opposed to love but is really the action of holy love in the face of evil. Love for those who are outcast often requires judgment against their oppressors.

3:1 Despite no apparent non-Christian evidence for the existence of this Nicodemus, the rabbinic writings do refer to two different men by that name, one generation on either side of Jesus' life. They are listed as part of the Gurion family and were wealthy, powerful, Phari-

from God as a teacher, for no one could perform these signs You do unless God were with him."

³ Jesus replied, "I assure you: Unless someone is born again,ᵃ he cannot see the kingdom of God."

TWISTED SCRIPTURE
John 3:3

*M*any who embrace reincarnation point to this verse and verse 7 ("You must be born again") to support their belief. But Jesus was speaking of a spiritual birth (v. 5), not a second physical birth (vv. 4-6).

⁴ "But how can anyone be born when he is old?" Nicodemus asked Him. "Can he enter his mother's womb a second time and be born?"

⁵ Jesus answered, "I assure you: Unless someone is born of water and the Spirit,ᵇ he cannot enter the kingdom of God. ⁶ Whatever is born of the flesh is flesh, and whatever is born of the Spirit is spirit. ⁷ Do not be amazed that I told you that youᶜ must be born again. ⁸ The windᵈ blows where it pleases, and you hear its sound, but you don't know where it comes from or where it is going. So it is with everyone born of the Spirit."

⁹ "How can these things be?" asked Nicodemus.

¹⁰ "Are you a teacherᵉ of Israel and don't know these things?" Jesus replied. ¹¹ "I assure you: We speak what We know and We testify to what We have seen, but youᶠ do not accept Our testimony.ᵍ ¹² If I have told you about things that happen on earth and you don't believe, how will you believe if I tell you about things of heaven? ¹³ No one has ascended into heaven except the One who descended from heaven—the Son of Man.ʰ ¹⁴ Just as Moses lifted up the snake in the wilderness, so the Son of Man must be lifted up, ¹⁵ so that everyone who believes in Him willⁱ have eternal life.

¹⁶ "For God loved the world in this way: He gave His One and Only Son, so that everyone who believes in Him will not perish but have eternal life. ¹⁷ For God did not send His Son into the world that He might condemn the world, but that the world might be saved through Him. ¹⁸ Anyone who believes in Him is not condemned, but anyone who does not believe is already condemned, because he has not believed in the name of the One and Only Son of God.

¹⁹ "This, then, is the judgment: the light

ᵃ3:3 The same Gk word can mean *again* or *from above* (also in v. 7). ᵇ3:5 Or *spirit*, or *wind*; the Gk word *pneuma* can mean *wind, spirit,* or *Spirit,* each of which occurs in this context. ᶜ3:7 The pronoun is pl in Gk. ᵈ3:8 The Gk word *pneuma* can mean *wind, spirit,* or *Spirit,* each of which occurs in this context. ᵉ3:10 Or *the teacher* ᶠ3:11 The word *you* in Gk is pl here and throughout v. 12. ᵍ3:11 The pl forms (*We, Our*) refer to Jesus and His authority to speak for the Father. ʰ3:13 Other mss add *who is in heaven* ⁱ3:15 Other mss add *not perish, but*

---

saic teachers—just like the character described here. Given the Jewish propensity for reusing favorite names, the name and attributes of this Nicodemus are entirely plausible.

3:2-9 Nicodemus started out so promisingly yet ended up not understanding Jesus at all. Is this conceivable for one who was called a teacher in Israel (v. 10)? Yes, and it was typical of the responses of various Jewish authorities to Jesus. John narrated a number of miracles ("signs") to try to convince people that Jesus was the Jewish Messiah (20:31), but he also recognized that signs by themselves can mislead (2:23-25). That John did not turn Nicodemus into a follower of Jesus (at least in this passage) contrasts with later Christian legends that did, making the historical plausibility of this episode all the greater.

3:3,7 It is sometimes argued that Jesus could not have said, "You must be born again," because this relies on a play on words between "born again" and "born from above" that works only in Greek, not in Aramaic. But whichever phrase Jesus used, He still clearly was talking about a second birth after a person's first, biological birth.

3:16 Muslims claim that God could not have a Son because they think Christians are talking about a literal biological offspring of the Father and Mary. However, throughout the NT, and especially in John, sonship refers to the intimate spiritual relationship between God and Jesus.

3:17 John said that Jesus didn't come to judge or condemn the world (12:47), but elsewhere we clearly read that Jesus will function as Judge on the last day, condemning some to hell (e.g., Mt 25:31-46). This is scarcely a contradiction, since John himself recorded that Jesus had all judgment entrusted to Him (Jn 5:22). The purpose of the incarnation was to offer a plan of salvation for all who would receive it. Those who refuse it simply remain in the condemned state they were already in. Or, in C. S. Lewis's words, "There are only two kinds of people in the end; those who say to God, 'Thy will be done,' and those to whom God says, 'Thy will be done.'"

*M*uslims do not believe that Jesus is the unique Son of God. According to the Koran, "No son did God beget, nor is there any God along with him" (Surah 23:91). But on nine occasions the Bible refers to Jesus as begotten of the Father. Not only did God declare Him to be His Son at His baptism (Lk 3:23), but also He proved it by raising Jesus from the dead (Rm 1:4).

has come into the world, and people loved darkness rather than the light because their deeds were evil. [20] For everyone who practices wicked things hates the light and avoids it,[a] so that his deeds may not be exposed. [21] But anyone who lives by[b] the truth comes to the light, so that his works may be shown to be accomplished by God." [c]

Jesus and John the Baptist

[22] After this, Jesus and His disciples went to the Judean countryside, where He spent time with them and baptized. [23] John also was baptizing in Aenon near Salim, because there was plenty of water there. People were coming and being baptized, [24] since John had not yet been thrown into prison.

[25] Then a dispute arose between John's disciples and a Jew[d] about purification. [26] So they came to John and told him, "Rabbi, the One you testified about, and who was with you across the Jordan, is baptizing—and everyone is flocking to Him."

[27] John responded, "No one can receive a

single thing unless it's given to him from heaven. [28] You yourselves can testify that I said, 'I am not the Messiah, but I've been sent ahead of Him.' [29] He who has the bride is the groom. But the groom's friend, who stands by and listens for him, rejoices greatly[e] at the groom's voice. So this joy of mine is complete. [30] He must increase, but I must decrease."

The One from Heaven

[31] The One who comes from above is above all. The one who is from the earth is earthly and speaks in earthly terms.[f] The One who comes from heaven is above all. [32] He testifies to what He has seen and heard, yet no one accepts His testimony. [33] The one who has accepted His testimony has affirmed that God is true. [34] For God sent Him, and He speaks God's words, since He[g] gives the Spirit without measure. [35] The Father loves the Son and has given all things into His hands. [36] The one who believes in the Son has eternal life, but the one who refuses to believe in the Son will not see life; instead, the wrath of God remains on him.

Jesus and the Samaritan Woman

4 When Jesus[h] knew that the Pharisees heard He was making and baptizing more disciples than John [2] (though Jesus Himself was not baptizing, but His disciples were), [3] He left Judea and went again to Galilee. [4] He had to travel through Samaria, [5] so He came to a town of Samaria

---

[a]3:20 Lit *and does not come to the light*   [b]3:21 Lit *who does*   [c]3:21 It is possible that Jesus' words end at v. 15. Ancient Gk did not have quotation marks.   [d]3:25 Other mss read *and the Jews*   [e]3:29 Lit *with joy rejoices*   [f]3:31 Or *of earthly things*   [g]3:34 Other mss read *since God*   [h]4:1 Other mss read *the Lord*

3:32 Here John made it sound as if no one ever accepted Jesus' testimony. Yet clearly Christ did gain followers. We must understand these words as a sweeping generalization about the growing reaction of Jesus' contemporaries. John was probably echoing Jesus' remark in verse 11 to Nicodemus: "You do not accept Our testimony," referring to the majority of the Jewish leaders.

4:1-2 Some have accused John of contradicting himself in the span of two verses by saying that Jesus baptized and then that He didn't. It is possible, however, that John penned verse 1 referring to Jesus and His followers together and then realized he needed to clarify

more precisely that it was the followers who performed the actual ritual. Given that John was more interested in contrasting Jesus and John the Baptist than in comparing them, his Gospel's comment that the two for a time had parallel ministries of baptism is not likely to be without historical foundation.

4:4 Jesus didn't have to go through Samaria. Jews in fact preferred to cross over and travel north on the eastern bank of the Jordan to avoid Samaria. But the compulsion was a theological one; it was God's will that Jesus go this way to have His appointed encounter with the woman at the well.

called Sychar near the property[a] that Jacob had given his son Joseph. [6] Jacob's well was there, and Jesus, worn out from His journey, sat down at the well. It was about six in the evening.[b]

[7] A woman of Samaria came to draw water.

"Give Me a drink," Jesus said to her, [8] for His disciples had gone into town to buy food.

[9] "How is it that You, a Jew, ask for a drink from me, a Samaritan woman?" she asked Him. For Jews do not associate with[c] Samaritans. [d]

[10] Jesus answered, "If you knew the gift of God, and who is saying to you, 'Give Me a drink,' you would ask Him, and He would give you living water."

[11] "Sir," said the woman, "You don't even have a bucket, and the well is deep. So where do You get this 'living water'? [12] You aren't greater than our father Jacob, are You? He gave us the well and drank from it himself, as did his sons and livestock."

[13] Jesus said, "Everyone who drinks from this water will get thirsty again. [14] But whoever drinks from the water that I will give him will never get thirsty again—ever! In fact, the water I will give him will become a well[e] of water springing up within him for eternal life."

[15] "Sir," the woman said to Him, "give me this water so I won't get thirsty and come here to draw water."

[16] "Go call your husband," He told her, "and come back here."

[17] "I don't have a husband," she answered.

"You have correctly said, 'I don't have a husband,'" Jesus said. [18] "For you've had five husbands, and the man you now have is not your husband. What you have said is true."

[19] "Sir," the woman replied, "I see that You are a prophet. [20] Our fathers worshiped on this mountain,[f] yet you ⌊Jews⌋ say that the place to worship is in Jerusalem."

[21] Jesus told her, "Believe Me, woman, an hour is coming when you will worship the Father neither on this mountain nor in Jerusalem. [22] You Samaritans[g] worship what you do not know. We worship what we do know, because salvation is from the Jews. [23] But an hour is coming, and is now here, when the true worshipers will worship the Father in spirit and truth. Yes, the Father wants such people to worship Him. [24] God is spirit, and those who worship Him must worship in spirit and truth."

[25] The woman said to Him, "I know that Messiah[h] is coming" (who is called Christ). "When He comes, He will explain everything to us."

[26] "I am ⌊He⌋," Jesus told her, "the One speaking to you."

The Ripened Harvest

[27] Just then His disciples arrived, and they were amazed that He was talking with a woman. Yet no one said, "What do You want?" or "Why are You talking with her?"

[28] Then the woman left her water jar, went into town, and told the men, [29] "Come, see a man who told me everything I ever did! Could this be the Messiah?" [30] They left the town and made their way to Him.

---

[a]4:5 Lit *piece of land* [b]4:6 Lit *the sixth hour*; see note at Jn 1:39; an alternate time reckoning would be *noon* [c]4:9 Or *do not share vessels with* [d]4:9 Other mss omit *For Jews do not associate with Samaritans.* [e]4:14 Or *spring* [f]4:20 Mount Gerizim, where there had been a Samaritan temple that rivaled Jerusalem's [g]4:22 *Samaritans* is implied since the Gk verb and pronoun are pl. [h]4:25 In the NT, the word Messiah translates the Gk word *Christos* ("Anointed One"), except here and in Jn 1:41 where it translates *Messias*.

4:9 Jews associated with Samaritans in numerous contexts, especially for commercial transactions. So either this is another sweeping generalization—Jews preferred to avoid Samaritans whenever they could—or the verb for "associate" should be translated "use the same dishes as," referring to the Jewish laws of ritual purity.

4:21-24 Verse 21 could sound like Jesus was discouraging worship anywhere, when in fact He was encourag-

ing it everywhere. No longer will there be one uniquely holy land or place in God's kingdom. On God as Spirit, see note on 1:18.

4:26 How could Jesus reveal Himself so plainly to this Samaritan woman when He was so coy with the Jewish leaders in Israel, especially as seen in the other three Gospels? Because the Samaritans were not looking for a militaristic ruler but expected a Messiah who would be more like a prophet and a teacher.

³¹ In the meantime the disciples kept urging Him, "Rabbi, eat something."

³² But He said, "I have food to eat that you don't know about."

³³ The disciples said to one another, "Could someone have brought Him something to eat?"

³⁴ "My food is to do the will of Him who sent Me and to finish His work," Jesus told them. ³⁵ "Don't you say, 'There are still four more months, then comes the harvest'? Listen ⌊to what⌋ I'm telling you: Open ᵃ your eyes and look at the fields, for they are ready ᵇ for harvest. ³⁶ The reaper is already receiving pay and gathering fruit for eternal life, so the sower and reaper can rejoice together. ³⁷ For in this case the saying is true: 'One sows and another reaps.' ³⁸ I sent you to reap what you

ᵃ4:35 Lit *Raise*   ᵇ4:35 Lit *white*

Can the Gospel Be Presented Across Cultures?

by John Mark Terry

ARTICLE

*E*vangelical Christians respond to this question with a resounding yes. The Bible includes many passages about cross-cultural evangelism. In the Great Commission (Mt 28:18-20), Jesus commanded His disciples to evangelize all the nations of the world. The word translated "nations" is the Greek word *ethne*, which is the root word for the English word *ethnic*. Thus Jesus instructed the apostles to make disciples of all the ethnic groups of the world. At His ascension (Ac 1), Jesus reiterated the command, instructing the apostles to witness even to the "ends of the earth" (Ac 1:8). Clearly the Bible reveals God's concern for all the cultures of the world.

Jesus Himself is the supreme example of cross-cultural ministry. Jesus left heaven to minister on earth. He was the first incarnational missionary as God in the flesh. In a similar way, Christians today should live the gospel among the cultures of the world. Jesus also demonstrated His concern for reaching other cultures by witnessing to the Samaritans, an ethnic group despised by the Jews of His day (Jn 4).

Peter, the leader of the early church, offers another example of cross-cultural ministry. Like most Jews of his day, he avoided contact with Gentiles. But through a vision God showed Peter the error of his prejudice, and Peter traveled to Caesarea to witness and stay in the home of Cornelius, a Roman army officer (Ac 10).

Paul provides a third example of cross-cultural witness. Though he had been raised to segregate himself from Gentiles, Paul met the Lord Jesus on the road to Damascus, and Christ called him to be a missionary to the Gentiles (Ac 9:15). Paul devoted the rest of his life to planting churches among Gentiles.

So the Bible clearly says that, yes, the gospel can be presented across cultural boundaries. Any doubt to the contrary is based upon the false contemporary assumption that at least some vital worldview beliefs (such as the gospel) are incommunicable to other cultures. This philosophical assumption has been shown to be false historically. In *A History of Christian Missions*, Bishop Stephen Neill wrote: "Christianity long has succeeded in making itself a universal religion." Bishop Neill said this doesn't mean that everyone has become a Christian, but Christians can be found in almost every country of the world—among "the most sophisticated of westerners to the aborigines of the inhospitable deserts of Australia."

didn't labor for; others have labored, and you have benefited from[a] their labor."

The Savior of the World

[39] Now many Samaritans from that town believed in Him because of what the woman said[b] when she testified, "He told me everything I ever did." [40] Therefore, when the Samaritans came to Him, they asked Him to stay with them, and He stayed there two days. [41] Many more believed because of what He said.[c] [42] And they told the woman, "We no longer believe because of what you said, for we have heard for ourselves and know that this really is the Savior of the world."[d]

A Galilean Welcome

[43] After two days He left there for Galilee. [44] Jesus Himself testified that a prophet has no honor in his own country. [45] When they entered Galilee, the Galileans welcomed Him because they had seen everything He did in Jerusalem during the festival. For they also had gone to the festival.

The Second Sign: Healing an Official's Son

[46] Then He went again to Cana of Galilee, where He had turned the water into wine. There was a certain royal official whose son was ill at Capernaum. [47] When this man heard that Jesus had come from Judea into Galilee, he went to Him and pleaded with Him to come down and heal his son, for he was about to die.

[48] Jesus told him, "Unless you ⌊people⌋ see signs and wonders, you will not believe."

[49] "Sir," the official said to Him, "come down before my boy dies!"

[50] "Go," Jesus told him, "your son will live." The man believed what[e] Jesus said to him and departed.

[51] While he was still going down, his slaves met him saying that his boy was alive. [52] He asked them at what time he got better. "Yesterday at seven in the morning[f] the fever left him," they answered. [53] The father realized this was the very hour at which Jesus had told him, "Your son will live." Then he himself believed, along with his whole household.

[54] This therefore was the second sign Jesus performed after He came from Judea to Galilee.

The Third Sign: Healing the Sick

After this, a Jewish festival took place, and Jesus went up to Jerusalem. [2] By the Sheep Gate in Jerusalem there is a pool, called Bethesda[g] in Hebrew, which has five colonnades.[h] [3] Within these lay a multitude of the sick—blind, lame, and paralyzed [—waiting for the moving of the water, [4] because an angel would go down into the pool from time to time and stir up the water. Then the first one who got in after the water was stirred up recovered from whatever ailment he had].[i]

[5] One man was there who had been sick for 38 years. [6] When Jesus saw him lying there and knew he had already been there a long time, He said to him, "Do you want to get well?"

[7] "Sir," the sick man answered, "I don't have a man to put me into the pool when the water is stirred up, but while I'm coming, someone goes down ahead of me."

[8] "Get up," Jesus told him, "pick up your

---

[a]4:38 Lit *you have entered into*   [b]4:39 Lit *because of the woman's word*   [c]4:41 Lit *because of His word*   [d]4:42 Other mss add *the Messiah*   [e]4:50 Lit *the word*   [f]4:52 Or *seven in the evening*; lit *at the seventh hour*; see note at Jn 1:39; an alternate time reckoning would be *at one in the afternoon*   [g]5:2 Other mss read *Bethzatha*; other mss read *Bethsaida*   [h]5:2 Rows of columns supporting a roof   [i]5:3–4 Other mss omit bracketed text

---

4:43-54 How does this episode fit with a similar miracle of healing in Mt 8:5-13 and Lk 7:1-10? It is hard to know for sure. On close examination there are no outright contradictions between the two, even though the Gospel writers have selected different portions to narrate. But they also may be two separate but similar incidents.

5:2 Until the 1890s, critics doubted this detail. Then the pool of Bethesda was excavated in Jerusalem and it turned out to have had five covered colonnades—four around the perimeter and one dividing the water into two compartments down the middle.

bedroll and walk!" [9] Instantly the man got well, picked up his bedroll, and started to walk.

Now that day was the Sabbath, [10] so the Jews said to the man who had been healed, "This is the Sabbath! It's illegal for you to pick up your bedroll."

[11] He replied, "The man who made me well told me, 'Pick up your bedroll and walk.' "

[12] "Who is this man who told you, 'Pick up ⌊your bedroll⌋ and walk?' " they asked. [13] But the man who was cured did not know who it was, because Jesus had slipped away into the crowd that was there. [a]

[14] After this, Jesus found him in the temple complex and said to him, "See, you are well. Do not sin any more, so that something worse doesn't happen to you." [15] The man went and reported to the Jews that it was Jesus who had made him well.

Honoring the Father and the Son

[16] Therefore, the Jews began persecuting Jesus [b] because He was doing these things on the Sabbath. [17] But Jesus responded to them, "My Father is still working, and I am working also." [18] This is why the Jews began trying all the more to kill Him: not only was He breaking the Sabbath, but He was even calling God His own Father, making Himself equal with God.

[19] Then Jesus replied, "I assure you: The Son is not able to do anything on His own, but only what He sees the Father doing. For whatever the Father [c] does, the Son also does these things in the same way. [20] For the Father loves the Son and shows Him everything He is doing, and He will show Him greater works than these so that you will be amazed. [21] And just as the Father raises the dead and gives them life, so the Son also gives life to anyone He wants to. [22] The Father, in fact, judges no one but has given all judgment to the Son, [23] so that all people will honor the Son just as they honor the Father. Anyone who does not honor the Son does not honor the Father who sent Him.

Life and Judgment

[24] "I assure you: Anyone who hears My word and believes Him who sent Me has eternal life and will not come under judgment but has passed from death to life.

[25] "I assure you: An hour is coming, and is now here, when the dead will hear the voice of the Son of God, and those who hear will live. [26] For just as the Father has life in Himself, so also He has granted to the Son to have life in Himself. [27] And He has granted Him the right to pass judgment, because He is the Son of Man. [28] Do not be amazed at this, because a time is coming when all who are in the graves will hear His voice [29] and come out—those who have done good things, to the resurrection of life, but those who have done wicked things, to the resurrection of judgment.

[30] "I can do nothing on My own. I judge only as I hear, and My judgment is righteous, because I do not seek My own will, but the will of Him who sent Me.

Four Witnesses to Jesus

[31] "If I testify about Myself, My testimony is not valid. [d] [32] There is Another who testi-

---

[a]5:13 Lit *slipped away, there being a crowd in that place*   [b]5:16 Other mss add *and trying to kill Him*   [c]5:19 Lit *whatever that One*   [d]5:31 Or *not true*

5:14 Sometimes this verse is used as a proof text for blaming all illness on someone's personal sin. But John contradicted this in 9:1-3. All Jesus was saying here was that this man's affliction seemed to have stemmed from some sin of his. Times of calamity are always good for personal stocktaking (Lk 13:1-9), but many tragedies are simply the results of life in a fallen world (Rm 8:22).

5:16-30 Throughout this passage it seems as if Jesus went back and forth between claiming He was equal to God and saying He was subordinate to His Father.

Actually, both were true. There was essential equality with functional subordination. All three persons of the Trinity are fully divine and united as one God in three persons, but they have distinct as well as overlapping roles. The Son never commands the Father; He only obeys Him.

5:31 Of course, Christ's testimony about Himself was valid because He spoke the truth. But Jesus was here alluding to the Jewish principle that self-witness was illegitimate on its own, so He went on to cite others who could testify on His behalf.

fies about Me, and I know that the testimony He gives about Me is valid.[a] [33] You have sent ⌊messengers⌋ to John, and he has testified to the truth. [34] I don't receive man's testimony, but I say these things so that you may be saved. [35] John[b] was a burning and shining lamp, and for a time you were willing to enjoy his light.

[36] "But I have a greater testimony than John's because of the works that the Father has given Me to accomplish. These very works I am doing testify about Me that the Father has sent Me. [37] The Father who sent Me has Himself testified about Me. You have not heard His voice at any time, and you haven't seen His form. [38] You don't have His word living in you, because you don't believe the One He sent. [39] You pore over[c] the Scriptures because you think you have eternal life in them, yet they testify about Me. [40] And you are not willing to come to Me that you may have life.

[41] "I do not accept glory from men, [42] but I know you—that you have no love for God within you. [43] I have come in My Father's name, yet you don't accept Me. If someone else comes in his own name, you will accept him. [44] How can you believe? While accepting glory from one another, you don't seek the glory that comes from the only God. [45] Do not think that I will accuse you to the Father. Your accuser is Moses, on whom you have set your hope. [46] For if you believed Moses, you would believe Me, because he wrote about Me. [47] But if you don't believe his writings, how will you believe My words?"

The Fourth Sign: Feeding 5,000

6 After this, Jesus crossed the Sea of Galilee (or Tiberias). [2] And a huge crowd was following Him because they saw the signs that He was performing on the sick. [3] So Jesus went up a mountain and sat down there with His disciples.

[4] Now the Passover, a Jewish festival, was near. [5] Therefore, when Jesus looked up and noticed a huge crowd coming toward Him, He asked Philip, "Where will we buy bread so these people can eat?" [6] He asked this to test him, for He Himself knew what He was going to do.

[7] Philip answered, "Two hundred denarii worth of bread wouldn't be enough for each of them to have a little."

[8] One of His disciples, Andrew, Simon Peter's brother, said to Him, [9] "There's a boy here who has five barley loaves and two fish—but what are they for so many?"

[10] Then Jesus said, "Have the people sit down."

There was plenty of grass in that place, so they sat down. The men numbered about 5,000. [11] Then Jesus took the loaves, and after giving thanks He distributed them to those who were seated—so also with the fish, as much as they wanted.

[12] When they were full, He told His disciples, "Collect the leftovers so that nothing is wasted." [13] So they collected them and filled 12 baskets with the pieces from the five barley loaves that were left over by those who had eaten.

[14] When the people saw the sign[d] He had done, they said, "This really is the Prophet who was to come into the world!" [15] Therefore, when Jesus knew that they were about to come and take Him by force to make Him king, He withdrew again[e] to the mountain by Himself.

The Fifth Sign: Walking on Water

[16] When evening came, His disciples went down to the sea, [17] got into a boat, and started

---

a5:32 Or *true* b5:35 Lit *That man* c5:39 In Gk this could be a command: *Pore over . . .* d6:14 Other mss read *signs* e6:15 A previous withdrawal is mentioned in Mk 6:31–32, an event that occurred just before the feeding of the 5,000.

6:14-15 In addition to specifying that it was Passover (v. 4), the attempt to make Jesus king was one of the distinctive features of John's account of the feeding of the 5,000. But even though these details do not appear in the other Gospels, many scholars (including some who are generally skeptical of John) accept them as accurate, because they fit so well the common Jewish misconception of the role of the Messiah and because no later Christian would likely have invented the unflattering picture of Jesus "running away" from would-be subjects of an earthly kingdom.

Are Jesus' Claims Unique Among the Religions of the World?

by Gary R. Habermas

*H*ave all major religious teachers proclaimed approximately the same message? For example, have many of the religious teachers taught that they were God, as Jesus did?

It may surprise many to learn that we have no reliable historical data that *any* of the founders of the world's major religions—apart from Jesus—ever claimed to be God. No early writings attest such a claim on behalf of these persons. For example, Chinese teachers Confucius and Lao-tzu exerted moral, social, and cultural influences on their students but were not theologians. Many of their wise sayings are reminiscent of the Hebrew book of Proverbs. Strangely, Buddha may have been an atheist who did not believe in any kind of divinity!

The Muslim holy book, the Qur'an, definitely does not elevate Muhammad to the place of Allah (God). While we are told that Muhammad is Allah's chief prophet, there is no attempt to make Muhammad deity. To the contrary, Allah has no partners (Surahs 4:171; 5:72, 116).

The OT places no leader or prophet on God's level. Rather, we are told that God will not share His glory with anyone else (Is 48:11). So Abraham, David, and Isaiah are not candidates for godhood.

Perhaps the Hindu figure Krishna comes closest to being understood as God. While he is referred to in the lofty terms of deity in the Hindu sacred writings, the Bhagavad-Gita (e.g., 4:13; 9:18-20,23), scholars are not sure whether Krishna ever really lived or, if he did, what century he lived in. Moreover, these writings do not claim to be historical treatises of any actual teachings and are thought to have been written hundreds of years after Krishna may have lived. Thus tracking any possibility of original claims is fruitless.

Further, being God in the usual Hindu sense would be quite distinct from the Judeo-Christian tradition. In the latter, God is by nature totally apart from His creation; humans do not reach godhood. In the Bhagavad-Gita, however, the process of enlightenment can be attained by those who return to the Godhead and achieve their own divinity (see 18:46-68). In a certain sense, all persons have divine natures.

On the contrary, Jesus claimed dual titles of divinity. Particularly, He said He was both the Son of God (Mt 11:27) and the Son of Man (Mk 2:10-11). He spoke of His Father in familiar ways (Mk 13:36) and even claimed to forgive sins, for which He was charged with blasphemy (Mk 2:5-7).

In perhaps the clearest indication of His claims about Himself, when the high priest asked Jesus if He was the Christ, the Son of God, Jesus plainly declared that He was. Then He further asserted that He was also the Son of Man who would co-reign on God's throne and come on the clouds in judgment. The high priest pronounced these claims blasphemy (Mk 14:61-64).

These sayings of Jesus were recorded in documents that were written just decades after the events, and there are strong reasons to hold that all were composed by authors who were close to the occurrences. Moreover, many of the individual passages exhibit earmarks of historicity. Last, very early creedal texts (e.g., Ac 2:36; Rm 1:3-4; 10:9) also apply titles of deity to Jesus Christ.

Many religious teachers have claimed to present God's way. But Jesus declared not only that He was initiating God's path of salvation (Mk 1:15-20) but also that what His hearers did specifically with *Him* determined their eternal destiny (Mt 10:37-40; 19:23-30). Further, of these religious founders, only Jesus taught that His death would serve as a payment for human sin, achieving what we could not (Mk 10:45; 14:22-25).

Additionally, only Jesus has miracles reported of Him by early sources. Most importantly, according to the Gospels, Jesus taught that His resurrection from the dead would be the sign that evidenced the truth of His message (Mt 12:38-42; 16:1-4; Mk 14:28). For NT writers, Jesus' resurrection proved His claims were true (Rm 1:3-4; 1 Pt 1:3-6). After all, dead men do not do much! So if Jesus was raised, God must have performed the event in order to approve Jesus' message (Ac 2:22-24; 17:30-31).

across the sea to Capernaum. Darkness had already set in, but Jesus had not yet come to them. [18] Then a high wind arose, and the sea began to churn. [19] After they had rowed about three or four miles,[a] they saw Jesus walking on the sea. He was coming near the boat, and they were afraid.

[20] But He said to them, "It is I.[b] Don't be afraid!" [21] Then they were willing to take Him on board, and at once the boat was at the shore where they were heading.

The Bread of Life

[22] The next day, the crowd that had stayed on the other side of the sea knew there had been only one boat.[c] [They also knew] that Jesus had not boarded the boat with His disciples, but that His disciples had gone off alone. [23] Some boats from Tiberias came near the place where they ate the bread after the Lord gave thanks. [24] When the crowd saw that neither Jesus nor His disciples were there, they got into the boats and went to Capernaum looking for Jesus.

[25] When they found Him on the other side of the sea, they said to Him, "Rabbi, when did You get here?"

[26] Jesus answered, "I assure you: You are looking for Me, not because you saw the signs, but because you ate the loaves and were filled. [27] Don't work for the food that perishes but for the food that lasts for eternal life, which the Son of Man will give you, because God the Father has set His seal of approval on Him."

[28] "What can we do to perform the works of God?" they asked.

[29] Jesus replied, "This is the work of God: that you believe in the One He has sent."

[30] "What sign then are You going to do so we may see and believe You?" they asked. "What are You going to perform? [31] Our fathers ate the manna in the wilderness, just as it is written: **He gave them bread from heaven to eat.**"[d] [e]

[32] Jesus said to them, "I assure you: Moses didn't give you the bread from heaven, but My Father gives you the real bread from

---

[a]6:19 Lit *25 or 30 stadia*; 1 *stadion* = 600 feet   [b]6:20 Lit *I am*   [c]6:22 Other mss add *into which His disciples had entered*   [d]6:31 Bread miraculously provided by God for the Israelites   [e]6:31 Ex 16:4; Ps 78:24

6:17 Mark 6:45 had the disciples set out for Bethsaida; John here said it was Capernaum. Yet if they were far enough to the northeast corner of the Sea of Galilee, then given the undulating northern coastline, both cities would have lain in a basically west-southwesterly direction of travel.

6:30 How could the crowds ask for anything be-

yond the feeding of the 5,000? In part, this was a different gathering, but more importantly, they were looking for someone to replicate the ongoing miracle of manna from heaven that had sustained the Israelites in the wilderness in the years after the exodus from Egypt (v. 31).

heaven. [33] For the bread of God is the One who comes down from heaven and gives life to the world."

[34] Then they said, "Sir, give us this bread always!"

[35] "I am the bread of life," Jesus told them. "No one who comes to Me will ever be hungry, and no one who believes in Me will ever be thirsty again. [36] But as I told you, you've seen Me,[a] and yet you do not believe. [37] Everyone the Father gives Me will come to Me, and the one who comes to Me I will never cast out. [38] For I have come down from heaven, not to do My will, but the will of Him who sent Me. [39] This is the will of Him who sent Me: that I should lose none of those He has given Me but should raise them up on the last day. [40] For this is the will of My Father: that everyone who sees the Son and believes in Him may have eternal life, and I will raise him up on the last day."

[41] Therefore the Jews started complaining about Him, because He said, "I am the bread that came down from heaven." [42] They were saying, "Isn't this Jesus the son of Joseph, whose father and mother we know? How can He now say, 'I have come down from heaven'?"

[43] Jesus answered them, "Stop complaining among yourselves. [44] No one can come to Me unless the Father who sent Me draws[b] him, and I will raise him up on the last day. [45] It is written in the Prophets: **And they will all be taught by God.**[c] Everyone who has listened to and learned from the Father comes to Me— [46] not that anyone has seen the Father except the One who is from God. He has seen the Father.

[47] "I assure you: Anyone who believes[d] has eternal life. [48] I am the bread of life. [49] Your fathers ate the manna in the wilderness, and they died. [50] This is the bread that comes down from heaven so that anyone may eat of it and not die. [51] I am the living bread that came down from heaven. If anyone eats of this bread he will live forever. The bread that I will give for the life of the world is My flesh."

[52] At that, the Jews argued among themselves, "How can this man give us His flesh to eat?"

[53] So Jesus said to them, "I assure you: Unless you eat the flesh of the Son of Man and drink His blood, you do not have life in yourselves. [54] Anyone who eats My flesh and drinks My blood has eternal life, and I will raise him up on the last day, [55] because My flesh is real food and My blood is real drink. [56] The one who eats My flesh and drinks My blood lives in Me, and I in him. [57] Just as the living Father sent Me and I live because of the Father, so the one who feeds on Me will live because of Me. [58] This is the bread that came down from heaven; it is not like the manna[e] your fathers ate—and they died. The one who eats this bread will live forever."

[59] He said these things while teaching in the synagogue in Capernaum.

Many Disciples Desert Jesus

[60] Therefore, when many of His disciples heard this, they said, "This teaching is hard! Who can accept[f] it?"

[61] Jesus, knowing in Himself that His disciples were complaining about this, asked them, "Does this offend you? [62] Then what if you were to observe the Son of Man ascending to where He was before? [63] The Spirit is the One who gives life. The flesh doesn't help at all. The words that I have spoken to you are spirit and are life. [64] But there are some

---

[a]6:36 Other mss omit *Me*   [b]6:44 Or *brings*, or *leads*; see the use of this Gk verb in Jn 12:32; 21:6; Ac 16:19; Jms 2:6.   [c]6:45 Is 54:13   [d]6:47 Other mss add *in Me*   [e]6:58 Other mss omit *the manna*   [f]6:60 Lit *hear*

6:52-59 Based on these verses, critics of the early church thought Christians condoned a form of cannibalism. This is not the case. The reference here is twofold, both foreshadowing the Lord's Supper and emphasizing complete submission to Jesus as Lord. To many insiders, it has seemed as if the Lord's Supper was a requirement for salvation. But verse 63 makes plain that only the Spirit gives life; Jesus' flesh does not do so. These are simply striking metaphors for identifying with Christ in His atoning death for the sins of humanity.

among you who don't believe." (For Jesus knew from the beginning those who would not[a] believe and the one who would betray Him.) [65] He said, "This is why I told you that no one can come to Me unless it is granted to him by the Father."

[66] From that moment many of His disciples turned back and no longer accompanied Him. [67] Therefore Jesus said to the Twelve, "You don't want to go away too, do you?"

[68] Simon Peter answered, "Lord, who will we go to? You have the words of eternal life. [69] We have come to believe and know that You are the Holy One of God!"[b]

[70] Jesus replied to them, "Didn't I choose you, the Twelve? Yet one of you is the Devil!" [71] He was referring to Judas, Simon Iscariot's son,[c] [d] one of the Twelve, because he was going to betray Him.

The Unbelief of Jesus' Brothers

After this, Jesus traveled in Galilee, since He did not want to travel in Judea because the Jews were trying to kill Him. [2] The Jewish Festival of Tabernacles[e] [f] was near, [3] so His brothers said to Him, "Leave here and go to Judea so Your disciples can see Your works that You are doing. [4] For no one does anything in secret while he's seeking public recognition. If You do these things, show Yourself to the world." [5] (For not even His brothers believed in Him.)

[6] Jesus told them, "My time has not yet ar-rived, but your time is always at hand. [7] The world cannot hate you, but it does hate Me because I testify about it—that its deeds are evil. [8] Go up to the festival yourselves. I'm not going up to the festival yet,[g] because My time has not yet fully come." [9] After He had said these things, He stayed in Galilee.

Jesus at the Festival of Tabernacles

[10] After His brothers had gone up to the festival, then He also went up, not openly but secretly. [11] The Jews were looking for Him at the festival and saying, "Where is He?" [12] And there was a lot of discussion about Him among the crowds. Some were saying, "He's a good man." Others were saying, "No, on the contrary, He's deceiving the people." [13] Still, nobody was talking publicly about Him because they feared the Jews.

[14] When the festival was already half over, Jesus went up into the temple complex and began to teach. [15] Then the Jews were amazed and said, "How does He know the Scriptures, since He hasn't been trained?"

[16] Jesus answered them, "My teaching isn't Mine but is from the One who sent Me. [17] If anyone wants to do His will, he will understand whether the teaching is from God or if I am speaking on My own. [18] The one who speaks for himself seeks his own glory. But He who seeks the glory of the One who sent Him is true, and there is no unrighteousness in Him. [19] Didn't Moses give you the law? Yet

---

[a]6:64 Other mss omit *not* [b]6:69 Other mss read *You are the Messiah, the Son of the Living God* [c]6:71 Other mss read *Judas Iscariot, Simon's son* [d]6:71 Lit *Judas, of Simon Iscariot* [e]7:2 Or *Booths* [f]7:2 One of 3 great Jewish religious festivals, along with Passover and Pentecost; Ex 23:14; Dt 16:16 [g]7:8 Other mss omit *yet*

6:68-69 It is not clear whether this is a drastically abbreviated version of the same conversation that the other Gospels narrate—Peter's confession on the road to Caesarea Philippi (Mt 16:16-20). More probably it is a forerunner of that later, more extensive conversation.

7:5 If Jesus was truly the Messiah who Christians claim He was, surely His own family members would have believed in Him? Not necessarily, especially if He had seemed like an ordinary boy when growing up. In fact, it's unlikely John would have reported this kind of skepticism if it weren't accurate. In the case of James, it may have taken a personal resurrection appearance to bring him to faith (1 Co 15:7).

7:8 The manuscripts vary as to whether John wrote the word "yet" before "going up to this Feast." But the

events imply that Jesus did not go immediately but rather waited until halfway through it before making His appearance (v. 14). As in His response to Mary at Cana (2:3-4), Jesus followed the Father's timing, not the commands of His own family.

7:15 If Jesus hadn't "been trained," does this mean He was illiterate or didn't have the detailed familiarity with Hebrew Scripture that the Gospels claim He did? No, He would have attended an elementary school of some sort in the synagogue, learned to read and write, and memorized much of the OT, like other Jewish boys between the ages of 5 and 12. But He had no formal, subsequent training with a rabbi that would qualify Him to act as an official rabbi.

none of you keeps the law! Why do you want to kill Me?"

[20] "You have a demon!" the crowd responded. "Who wants to kill You?"

[21] "I did one work, and you are all amazed," Jesus answered. [22] "Consider this: Moses has given you circumcision—not that it comes from Moses but from the fathers—and you circumcise a man on the Sabbath. [23] If a man receives circumcision on the Sabbath so that the law of Moses won't be broken, are you angry at Me because I made a man entirely well on the Sabbath? [24] Stop judging according to outward appearances; rather judge according to righteous judgment."

The Identity of the Messiah

[25] Some of the people of Jerusalem were saying, "Isn't this the man they want to kill? [26] Yet, look! He's speaking publicly and they're saying nothing to Him. Can it be true that the authorities know He is the Messiah? [27] But we know where this man is from. When the Messiah comes, nobody will know where He is from."

[28] As He was teaching in the temple complex, Jesus cried out, "You know Me and you know where I am from. Yet I have not come on My own, but the One who sent Me is true. You don't know Him; [29] I know Him because I am from Him, and He sent Me."

[30] Then they tried to seize Him. Yet no one laid a hand on Him because His hour[a] had not yet come. [31] However, many from the crowd believed in Him and said, "When the Messiah comes, He won't perform more signs than this man has done, will He?"

[32] The Pharisees heard the crowd muttering these things about Him, so the chief priests and the Pharisees sent temple police to arrest Him.

[33] Then Jesus said, "I am only with you for a short time. Then I'm going to the One who sent Me. [34] You will look for Me, but you will not find Me; and where I am, you cannot come."

[35] Then the Jews said to one another, "Where does He intend to go so we won't find Him? He doesn't intend to go to the Dispersion[b] among the Greeks and teach the Greeks, does He? [36] What is this remark He made: 'You will look for Me, and you will not find Me; and where I am, you cannot come'?"

The Promise of the Spirit

[37] On the last and most important day of the festival, Jesus stood up and cried out, "If anyone is thirsty, he should come to Me[c] and drink! [38] The one who believes in Me, as the Scripture has said,[d] will have streams of living water flow from deep within him." [39] He said this about the Spirit, whom those who believed in Him were going to receive, for the Spirit[e] had not yet been received,[f][g] because Jesus had not yet been glorified.

The People Are Divided over Jesus

[40] When some from the crowd heard these words, they said, "This really is the Prophet!"[h] [41] Others said, "This is the Messiah!" But

---

[a]7:30 The time of His sacrificial death and exaltation; Jn 2:4; 8:20; 12:23,27; 13:1; 17:1 [b]7:35 Jewish people scattered throughout Gentile lands who spoke Gk and were influenced by Gk culture [c]7:37 Other mss omit *to Me* [d]7:38 Jesus may have had several OT passages in mind; Is 58:11; Ezk 47:1–12; Zch 14:8 [e]7:39 Other mss read *Holy Spirit* [f]7:39 Other mss read *had not yet been given* [g]7:39 Lit *the Spirit was not yet*; the word *received* is implied from the previous clause. [h]7:40 Probably = the Prophet in Dt 18:15

7:27 If no one was supposed to know where the Messiah came from, how could Jesus—born in Bethlehem and raised in Nazareth—qualify? Actually, the Jewish belief that the Messiah would emerge "out of nowhere" was a tradition with no OT support. That said, it is true that the skeptics didn't know where Jesus truly came from—i.e., from God (v. 28).

7:34-36 How do we answer the authorities' question about Jesus' claim to be going away where no one could find Him? By understanding Him to have been referring to His death, resurrection, and ascension. They would look for Him later, but physically they would not be able to find Him. His Holy Spirit would be with His followers (see 8:21-22).

7:39 The Holy Spirit had been given frequently, but only temporarily, to various people throughout the OT. But He would permanently indwell God's people only after Jesus' death and exaltation (14:17; cp. Ac 2).

7:41-42,52 These verses do not contradict Mt 2:1 and Lk 2:4 on Jesus' being born in Bethlehem. Rather, they point out (ironically) how Jesus was rejected because some said, "Surely the Messiah doesn't come from Galilee, does He? [42] Doesn't the Scripture say that the Messiah comes from David's offspring[a] and from the town of Bethlehem, where David once lived?" [43] So a division occurred among the crowd because of Him. [44] Some of them wanted to seize Him, but no one laid hands on Him.

Debate over Jesus' Claims

[45] Then the temple police came to the chief priests and Pharisees, who asked them, "Why haven't you brought Him?"

[46] The police answered, "No man ever spoke like this!"[b]

[47] Then the Pharisees responded to them: "Are you fooled too? [48] Have any of the rulers believed in Him? Or any of the Pharisees? [49] But this crowd, which doesn't know the law, is accursed!"

[50] Nicodemus—the one who came to Him previously, being one of them—said to them, [51] "Our law doesn't judge a man before it hears from him and knows what he's doing, does it?"

[52] "You aren't from Galilee too, are you?" they replied. "Investigate and you will see that no prophet arises from Galilee."[c]

8 [[53] So each one went to his house. [1] But Jesus went to the Mount of Olives.

An Adulteress Forgiven

[2] At dawn He went to the temple complex again, and all the people were coming to Him. He sat down and began to teach them. [3] Then the scribes and the Pharisees brought a woman caught in adultery, making her stand in the center. [4] "Teacher," they said to Him, "this woman was caught in the act of committing adultery. [5] In the law Moses commanded us to stone such women. So what do You say?" [6] They asked this to trap Him, in order that they might have evidence to accuse Him.

Jesus stooped down and started writing on the ground with His finger. [7] When they persisted in questioning Him, He stood up and said to them, "The one without sin among you should be the first to throw a stone at her."

[8] Then He stooped down again and continued writing on the ground. [9] When they heard this, they left one by one, starting with the older men. Only He was left, with the woman in the center. [10] When Jesus stood up, He said to her, "Woman, where are they? Has no one condemned you?"

[11] "No one, Lord,"[d] she answered.

"Neither do I condemn you," said Jesus. "Go, and from now on do not sin any more."][e]

The Light of the World

[12] Then Jesus spoke to them again: "I am the light of the world. Anyone who follows Me will never walk in the darkness but will have the light of life."

[13] So the Pharisees said to Him, "You are testifying about Yourself. Your testimony is not valid."[f]

[14] "Even if I testify about Myself," Jesus replied, "My testimony is valid,[g] because I know where I came from and where I'm going. But you don't know where I come from or where I'm going. [15] You judge by human standards.[h] I judge no one. [16] And if I do

---

[a]7:42 Lit seed [b]7:46 Other mss read like this man [c]7:52 Jonah and probably other prophets did come from Galilee; 2 Kg 14:25 [d]8:11 Or Sir; Jn 4:15,49; 5:7; 6:34; 9:36 [e]8:11 Other mss omit bracketed text [f]8:13 The law of Moses required at least 2 witnesses to make a claim legally valid (v. 17). [g]8:14 Or true [h]8:15 Lit You judge according to the flesh

---

people mistakenly think He was born in Nazareth, where He grew up. Some prophets did in fact come from Galilee (Hosea, Jonah, Nahum), but not "the Prophet"—i.e., the Messiah, as the textual variant clarifies.

7:53–8:11 This event is not found in the oldest and best manuscripts, It is, however, widely believed to be a true story about Jesus that was preserved in the oral tradition and eventually added by well-meaning scribes.

8:14 Earlier Jesus accepted, for the sake of argument, the Jewish belief that self-testimony was illegitimate (5:31). Here He pointed out explicitly what had been true all along, that He did in fact tell the truth about Himself, whether or not anyone else supported Him. And in verse 18 He did go on to provide another witness.

8:15-16 Jesus was not contradicting Himself in the span of two verses—first not judging, then judging. Rather,

judge, My judgment is true, because I am not alone, but I and the Father who sent Me ⌊judge together⌋. *17* Even in your law it is written that the witness of two men is valid. *18* I am the One who testifies about Myself, and the Father who sent Me testifies about Me."

19 Then they asked Him, "Where is Your Father?"

"You know neither Me nor My Father," Jesus answered. "If you knew Me, you would also know My Father." *20* He spoke these words by the treasury,ª while teaching in the temple complex. But no one seized Him, because His hourᵇ had not come.

Jesus Predicts His Departure

21 Then He said to them again, "I'm going away; you will look for Me, and you will die in your sin. Where I'm going, you cannot come."

22 So the Jews said again, "He won't kill Himself, will He, since He says, 'Where I'm going, you cannot come'?"

23 "You are from below," He told them, "I am from above. You are of this world; I am not of this world. *24* Therefore I told you that you will die in your sins. For if you do not believe that I am ⌊He⌋,ᶜ you will die in your sins."

25 "Who are You?" they questioned.

"Precisely what I've been telling you from the very beginning," Jesus told them. *26* "I have many things to say and to judge about you, but the One who sent Me is true, and what I have heard from Him—these things I tell the world."

27 They did not know He was speaking to them about the Father. *28* So Jesus said to them, "When you lift up the Son of Man, then you will know that I am ⌊He⌋, and that I do nothing on My own. But just as the Father taught Me, I say these things. *29* The One who sent Me is with Me. He has not left Me alone, because I always do what pleases Him."

Truth and Freedom

30 As He was saying these things, many believed in Him. *31* So Jesus said to the Jews who had believed Him, "If you continue in My word,ᵈ you really are My disciples. *32* You will know the truth, and the truth will set you free."

33 "We are descendantsᵉ of Abraham," they answered Him, "and we have never been enslaved to anyone. How can You say, 'You will become free'?"

34 Jesus responded, "I assure you: Everyone who commits sin is a slave of sin. *35* A slave does not remain in the household forever, but a son does remain forever. *36* Therefore if the Son sets you free, you really will be free. *37* I know you are descendantsᵉ of Abraham, but you are trying to kill Me because My wordᵈ is not welcome among you. *38* I speak what I have seen in the presence of the Father,ᶠ and therefore you do what you have heard from your father."

39 "Our father is Abraham!" they replied.

"If you were Abraham's children," Jesus told them, "you would do what Abraham did. *40* But now you are trying to kill Me, a man who has told you the truth that I heard from God. Abraham did not do this! *41* You're doing what your father does."

"We weren't born of sexual immorality," they said. "We have one Father—God."

ª8:20 A place for offerings to be given, perhaps in the court of women   ᵇ8:20 The time of His sacrificial death and exaltation; Jn 2:4; 7:30; 12:23,27; 13:1; 17:1   ᶜ8:24 Jesus claimed to be deity, but the Pharisees didn't understand His meaning.   ᵈ8:31,37 Or *My teaching*, or *My message*   ᵉ8:33,37 Or *offspring*; lit *seed*; Jn 7:42   ᶠ8:38 Other mss read *of My Father*

He passed judgment on no one of His own accord; His judgment was always mirroring the Father's judgment (v. 16).

8:30-59 In verses 30-31, various listeners seem to have believed in Jesus, but by the end of the chapter they were ready to stone Him. As verse 31 stresses, appearance of belief must be matched by perseverance in following Jesus and His teaching. Much of the belief attested to in verse 30 was probably superficial. There may also have been a narrowing of the audience Jesus was addressing, starting in verse 48—"the Jews" here may include some of the authorities who had never claimed to believe in Him at any level.

8:33 Of course the Jews had frequently been slaves—in Egypt, Assyria, Babylon, and Persia as well as under Greece and now under Rome. Presumably they were claiming here that they were never spiritually enslaved.

⁴² Jesus said to them, "If God were your Father, you would love Me, because I came from God and I am here. For I didn't come on My own, but He sent Me. ⁴³ Why don't you understand what I say? Because you cannot listen to ª My word. ⁴⁴ You are of your father the Devil, and you want to carry out your father's desires. He was a murderer from the beginning and has not stood in the truth, because there is no truth in him. When he tells a lie, he speaks from his own nature,ᵇ because he is a liar and the father of liars.ᶜ ⁴⁵ Yet because I tell the truth, you do not believe Me. ⁴⁶ Who among you can convict Me of sin? If I tell the truth, why don't you believe Me? ⁴⁷ The one who is from God listens to God's words. This is why you don't listen, because you are not from God."

Jesus and Abraham

⁴⁸ The Jews responded to Him, "Aren't we right in saying that You're a Samaritan and have a demon?"

⁴⁹ "I do not have a demon," Jesus answered. "On the contrary, I honor My Father and you dishonor Me. ⁵⁰ I do not seek My glory; the One who seeks it also judges. ⁵¹ I assure you: If anyone keeps My word, he will never see death—ever!"

⁵² Then the Jews said, "Now we know You have a demon. Abraham died and so did the prophets. You say, 'If anyone keeps My word, he will never taste death—ever!' ⁵³ Are You greater than our father Abraham who died? Even the prophets died. Who do You pretend to be?"ᵈ

⁵⁴ "If I glorify Myself," Jesus answered, "My glory is nothing. My Father—you say about Him, 'He is our God'—He is the One who glorifies Me. ⁵⁵ You've never known Him, but I know Him. If I were to say I don't know Him, I would be a liar like you. But I do know Him, and I keep His word. ⁵⁶ Your father Abraham was overjoyed that he would see My day; he saw it and rejoiced."

⁵⁷ The Jews replied, "You aren't 50 years old yet, and You've seen Abraham?"ᵉ

⁵⁸ Jesus said to them, "I assure you: Before Abraham was, I am."ᶠ

⁵⁹ At that, they picked up stones to throw at Him. But Jesus was hidden ᵍ and went out of the temple complex.ʰ

The Sixth Sign: Healing a Man Born Blind

9 As He was passing by, He saw a man blind from birth. ² His disciples questioned Him: "Rabbi, who sinned, this man or his parents, that he was born blind?"

³ "Neither this man nor his parents sinned," Jesus answered. "₍This came about₎ so that God's works might be displayed in him. ⁴ We ⁱ must do the works of Him who sent Me ʲ

TWISTED SCRIPTURE
John 9:2

This verse, when twisted, seems to support reincarnation. The implication is that in a previous life the man sinned and was thus born blind in the next life. The reference, however, is to a Jewish belief that a fetus could commit a sin while in his mother's womb. The concept of reincarnation was foreign to Hebrew thought. Jews believed in resurrection, not reincarnation.

ᵃ8:43 Or *cannot hear* ᵇ8:44 Lit *from his own things* ᶜ8:44 Lit *of it* ᵈ8:53 Lit *Who do You make Yourself?* ᵉ8:57 Other mss read *and Abraham has seen You?* ᶠ8:58 *I AM* is the name God gave Himself at the burning bush; Ex 3:13–14; see note at Jn 8:24. ᵍ8:59 Or *Jesus hid Himself* ʰ8:59 Other mss add *and having gone through their midst, He passed by* ⁱ9:4 Other mss read *I* ʲ9:4 Other mss read *sent us*

8:44 Surely this was the height of anti-Semitism? Actually, Jesus was calling only one specific group of Jews sons of the devil. Jesus was a Jew, as were all His first followers. The OT prophetic books contain many equally sharp rebukes (e.g., Jr 9:7-9), and they are certainly not anti-Semitic.

8:58 This is not bad grammar but an allusion to the divine name "I AM" of Yahweh, God of Israel (Ex 3:14). The Greek text uses the present tense, and thus the Jehovah's Witnesses' New World Translation is wrong to render it, "I have been," as if Jesus were claiming only to have existed some time before Abraham.

9:1-3 If 5:14 is taken to mean that all sick and disabled persons are being punished for their own sin, then we have a contradiction. Rather, this incident shows that 5:14 cannot be made a universal principle. Often God has specific purposes in allowing His people to remain unwell (2 Co 12:9). In this case, God will grant healing, but primarily to bring Himself the glory.

while it is day. Night is coming when no one can work. [5] As long as I am in the world, I am the light of the world."

[6] After He said these things He spit on the ground, made some mud from the saliva, and spread the mud on his eyes. [7] "Go," He told him, "wash in the pool of Siloam" (which means "Sent"). So he left, washed, and came back seeing.

[8] His neighbors and those who formerly had seen him as a beggar said, "Isn't this the man who sat begging?" [9] Some said, "He's the one." "No," others were saying, "but he looks like him."

He kept saying, "I'm the one!"

[10] Therefore they asked him, "Then how were your eyes opened?"

[11] He answered, "The man called Jesus made mud, spread it on my eyes, and told me, 'Go to Siloam and wash.' So when I went and washed I received my sight."

[12] "Where is He?" they asked.

"I don't know," he said.

The Healed Man's Testimony

[13] They brought the man who used to be blind to the Pharisees. [14] The day that Jesus made the mud and opened his eyes was a Sabbath. [15] So again the Pharisees asked him how he received his sight.

"He put mud on my eyes," he told them. "I washed and I can see."

[16] Therefore some of the Pharisees said, "This man is not from God, for He doesn't keep the Sabbath!" But others were saying, "How can a sinful man perform such signs?" And there was a division among them.

[17] Again they asked the blind man,[a] "What do you say about Him, since He opened your eyes?"

"He's a prophet," he said.

[18] The Jews did not believe this about him—that he was blind and received sight—until they summoned the parents of the one who had received his sight.

[19] They asked them, "Is this your son, [the one] you say was born blind? How then does he now see?"

[20] "We know this is our son and that he was born blind," his parents answered. [21] "But we don't know how he now sees, and we don't know who opened his eyes. Ask him; he's of age. He will speak for himself." [22] His parents said these things because they were afraid of the Jews, since the Jews had already agreed that if anyone confessed Him as Messiah, he would be banned from the synagogue. [23] This is why his parents said, "He's of age; ask him."

[24] So a second time they summoned the man who had been blind and told him, "Give glory to God.[b] We know that this man is a sinner!"

[25] He answered, "Whether or not He's a sinner, I don't know. One thing I do know: I was blind, and now I can see!"

[26] Then they asked him, "What did He do to you? How did He open your eyes?"

[27] "I already told you," he said, "and you didn't listen. Why do you want to hear it again? You don't want to become His disciples too, do you?"

[28] They ridiculed him: "You're that man's disciple, but we're Moses' disciples. [29] We know that God has spoken to Moses. But this man—we don't know where He's from!"

[30] "This is an amazing thing," the man told them. "You don't know where He is from, yet He opened my eyes! [31] We know that God doesn't listen to sinners, but if anyone is

---

[a]9:17 = the man who had been blind   [b]9:24 *Give glory to God* was a solemn charge to tell the truth; Jos 7:19.

9:6-7 Here and in Mk 7:33-35 Jesus used saliva rather than just His spoken word in healing someone. Spittle was often believed to have medicinal value in the ancient world. God can heal directly or through all kinds of indirect means, including modern medicine (and, occasionally, mud packs). The pool of Siloam is another location, once doubted, that archaeology has confirmed.

9:22; 12:42; 16:2 It is often alleged that these three verses anachronistically refer to a later Jewish practice of excommunicating synagogue members who became followers of Jesus. But even then the practice was at best only sporadic throughout the empire. Indeed, John's references may not refer to anything more widespread than a policy in Jerusalem, precisely where such persecution would have started at a very early date (Ac 4–5).

God-fearing and does His will, He listens to him. [32] Throughout history[a] no one has ever heard of someone opening the eyes of a person born blind. [33] If this man were not from God, He wouldn't be able to do anything."

[34] "You were born entirely in sin," they replied, "and are you trying to teach us?" Then they threw him out. [b]

The Blind Man's Sight and the Pharisees' Blindness

[35] When Jesus heard that they had thrown the man out, He found him and asked, "Do you believe in the Son of Man?"[c]

[36] "Who is He, Sir, that I may believe in Him?" he asked.

[37] Jesus answered, "You have seen Him; in fact, He is the One speaking with you."

[38] "I believe, Lord!" he said, and he worshiped Him.

[39] Jesus said, "I came into this world for judgment, in order that those who do not see will see and those who do see will become blind."

[40] Some of the Pharisees who were with Him heard these things and asked Him, "We aren't blind too, are we?"

[41] "If you were blind," Jesus told them, "you wouldn't have sin.[d] But now that you say, 'We see'—your sin remains.

The Ideal Shepherd

10 "I assure you: Anyone who doesn't enter the sheep pen by the door but climbs in some other way, is a thief and a robber. [2] The one who enters by the door is the shepherd of the sheep. [3] The doorkeeper opens it for him, and the sheep hear his voice. He calls his own sheep by name and leads them out. [4] When he has brought all his own outside, he goes ahead of them. The sheep follow him because they recognize his voice. [5] They will never follow a stranger; instead they will run away from him, because they don't recognize the voice of strangers."

[6] Jesus gave them this illustration, but they did not understand what He was telling them.

The Good Shepherd

[7] So Jesus said again, "I assure you: I am the door of the sheep. [8] All who came before Me[e] are thieves and robbers, but the sheep didn't listen to them. [9] I am the door. If anyone enters by Me, he will be saved and will come in and go out and find pasture. [10] A thief comes only to steal and to kill and to destroy. I have come that they may have life and have it in abundance.

[11] "I am the good shepherd. The good shepherd lays down his life for the sheep. [12] The hired man, since he is not the shepherd and doesn't own the sheep, leaves them[f] and runs away when he sees a wolf coming. The wolf then snatches and scatters them. [13] ⌊This happens⌋ because he is a hired man and doesn't care about the sheep.

[14] "I am the good shepherd. I know My own sheep, and they know Me, [15] as the Father knows Me, and I know the Father. I lay down My life for the sheep. [16] But I have other

---

[a]9:32 Lit *From the age* [b]9:34 = they banned him from the synagogue; v. 22 [c]9:35 Other mss read *the Son of God* [d]9:41 To *have sin* is an idiom that refers to guilt caused by sin. [e]10:8 Other mss omit *before Me* [f]10:12 Lit *leaves the sheep*

9:33 Like Gamaliel's advice to the Sanhedrin later (Ac 5:38), this man's logic is not watertight. Satan can counterfeit many miracles. But God providentially used this reasoning to help the man come to faith in this situation. The trustworthiness of Scripture does not mean that every human opinion narrated is true, just that those opinions have been accurately reported.

9:41 All people are sinners, but if these Pharisees acknowledged their spiritual blindness, they would not be guilty of the specific sin of claiming to be innocent when they were not.

10:8 "All who came before Me" obviously cannot refer to godly leaders in OT times. Note that the text says "are thieves and robbers" (as in the Gk), which may suggest that Jesus had just His contemporaries in view.

10:10 In context, this is no promise of health, wealth, or easy living by worldly standards. The abundant Christian life means salvation (v. 9); in this world, however, it may involve martyrdom (15:13).

10:16 When Jesus addressed Jews and spoke about "other sheep," He would have had Gentiles in mind. His church would unite Jew and Gentile (Gl 3:28). There

sheep that are not of this fold; I must bring them also, and they will listen to My voice. Then there will be one flock, one shepherd. [17] This is why the Father loves Me, because I am laying down My life so I may take it up again. [18] No one takes it from Me, but I lay it down on My own. I have the right to lay it down, and I have the right to take it up again. I have received this command from My Father."

[19] Again a division took place among the Jews because of these words. [20] Many of them were saying, "He has a demon and He's crazy! Why do you listen to Him?" [21] Others were saying, "These aren't the words of someone demon-possessed. Can a demon open the eyes of the blind?"

Jesus at the Festival of Dedication

[22] Then the Festival of Dedication[a] took place in Jerusalem, and it was winter. [23] Jesus was walking in the temple complex in Solomon's Colonnade.[b] [24] Then the Jews surrounded Him and asked, "How long are You going to keep us in suspense?[c] If You are the Messiah, tell us plainly."[d]

[25] "I did tell you and you don't believe," Jesus answered them. "The works that I do in My Father's name testify about Me. [26] But you don't believe because you are not My sheep.[e] [27] My sheep hear My voice, I know them, and they follow Me. [28] I give them eternal life, and they will never perish—ever! No one will snatch them out of My hand. [29] My Father, who has given them to Me, is greater than all. No one is able to snatch them out

of the Father's hand. [30] The Father and I are one."[f]

Renewed Efforts to Stone Jesus

[31] Again the Jews picked up rocks to stone Him.

[32] Jesus replied, "I have shown you many good works from the Father. Which of these works are you stoning Me for?"

[33] "We aren't stoning You for a good work," the Jews answered, "but for blasphemy, because You—being a man—make Yourself God."

[34] Jesus answered them, "Isn't it written in your law,[g] **I said, you are gods**?[h] [35] If He called those whom the word of God came to 'gods'—and the Scripture cannot be broken— [36] do you say, 'You are blaspheming' to the One the Father set apart and sent into

TWISTED SCRIPTURE
John 10:34

An assortment of New Age sects and quasi-Christian cults believe that humans are divine. Often they point to this verse as support. This verse is actually a reference to Ps 82:6, a psalm of Asaph, which describes OT judges who stand in the place of God to judge His people. Being His representatives, they possess delegated authority to speak on His behalf. In Ps 82:7 these gods/judges are said to face death because of their unjust verdicts, showing conclusively that they are human and not divine beings. The word translated "gods" (*elohim*) in Ps 82:6 is translated "judges" in Ex 21:6 and 22:8.

[a]10:22 Or *Hanukkah*, also called *the Feast of Lights*; this festival commemorated the rededication of the temple in 164 B.C.   [b]10:23 Rows of columns supporting a roof   [c]10:24 Lit *How long are you taking away our life?*   [d]10:24 Or *openly*, or *publicly*   [e]10:26 Other mss add *just as I told you*   [f]10:30 Lit *I and the Father—We are one.*   [g]10:34 Other mss read *in the law*   [h]10:34 Ps 82:6

is no reason to believe the Mormon claim that He was speaking here of Native Americans and an appearance in the New World.

10:24 This verse is a good reminder that all of Jesus' "I am" statements—"bread of life," "light of the world," etc.—were primarily metaphors. They were not intended to be unambiguous revelations of His deity, as they seem to Christians today with "20/20 hindsight."

10:30 Jesus' claims to be one with God transgressed boundaries that some Jewish authorities believed no human should ever cross, lest one be arrogating to

himself divine prerogatives. That some wanted to stone Jesus (vv. 31-33) shows that His was more than a claim to be one with God in mind, will, or purpose.

10:34-36 This is not an acknowledgement of polytheism or a claim that human beings are gods; it is an argument "from the lesser to the greater." Human judges in Israel were called "gods" because of their exalted (though abused) roles in Ps 82:6, so it could not automatically have been blasphemy for Jesus to refer to Himself as God's Son.

the world, because I said: I am the Son of God? [37] If I am not doing My Father's works, don't believe Me. [38] But if I am doing them and you don't believe Me, believe the works. This way you will know and understand[a] that the Father is in Me and I in the Father." [39] Then they were trying again to seize Him, yet He eluded their grasp.

Many beyond the Jordan Believe in Jesus

[40] So He departed again across the Jordan to the place where John had been baptizing earlier, and He remained there. [41] Many came to Him and said, "John never did a sign, but everything John said about this man was true." [42] And many believed in Him there.

Lazarus Dies at Bethany

11 Now a man was sick, Lazarus, from Bethany, the village of Mary and her sister Martha. [2] Mary was the one who anointed the Lord with fragrant oil and wiped His feet with her hair, and it was her brother Lazarus who was sick. [3] So the sisters sent a message to Him: "Lord, the one You love is sick."

[4] When Jesus heard it, He said, "This sickness will not end in death but is for the glory of God, so that the Son of God may be glorified through it." [5] (Jesus loved Martha, her sister, and Lazarus.) [6] So when He heard that he was sick, He stayed two more days in the place where He was. [7] Then after that, He said to the disciples, "Let's go to Judea again."

[8] "Rabbi," the disciples told Him, "just now the Jews tried to stone You, and You're going there again?"

[9] "Aren't there 12 hours in a day?" Jesus answered. "If anyone walks during the day, he doesn't stumble, because he sees the light of this world. [10] If anyone walks during the night, he does stumble, because the light is not in him." [11] He said this, and then He told them, "Our friend Lazarus has fallen asleep, but I'm on My way to wake him up."

[12] Then the disciples said to Him, "Lord, if he has fallen asleep, he will get well."

[13] Jesus, however, was speaking about his death, but they thought He was speaking about natural sleep. [14] So Jesus then told them plainly, "Lazarus has died. [15] I'm glad for you that I wasn't there so that you may believe. But let's go to him."

[16] Then Thomas (called "Twin") said to his fellow disciples, "Let's go so that we may die with Him."

The Resurrection and the Life

[17] When Jesus arrived, He found that Lazarus had already been in the tomb four days. [18] Bethany was near Jerusalem (about two miles[b] away). [19] Many of the Jews had come to Martha and Mary to comfort them about their brother. [20] As soon as Martha heard that Jesus was coming, she went to meet Him. But Mary remained seated in the house.

[21] Then Martha said to Jesus, "Lord, if You had been here, my brother wouldn't have died. [22] Yet even now I know that whatever You ask from God, God will give You."

[23] "Your brother will rise again," Jesus told her.

[24] Martha said, "I know that he will rise again in the resurrection at the last day."

[25] Jesus said to her, "I am the resurrection and the life. The one who believes in Me, even if he dies, will live. [26] Everyone who lives and believes in Me will never die—ever. Do you believe this?"

[27] "Yes, Lord," she told Him, "I believe You are the Messiah, the Son of God, who was to come into the world."

---

[a]10:38 Other mss read *know and believe*   [b]11:18 Lit *15 stadia*; 1 *stadion* = 600 feet

11:6,37 Jesus did not contradict His love for Lazarus (v. 5) by delaying His departure. Instead, Jesus magnified the miracle of raising someone four days dead, and God received even more glory (vv. 4,15). Thematically, John used this miracle as an implied response to the question Jesus posed in 10:36.

11:27,39 There was no Jewish tradition of anyone being resurrected apart from or in advance of the general resurrection of all people on the last day. So Martha could easily hold this view (v. 24), believe in Jesus (v. 27), and still not expect Lazarus to be raised on the spot (v. 39).

Jesus Shares the Sorrow of Death

[28] Having said this, she went back and called her sister Mary, saying in private, "The Teacher is here and is calling for you."

[29] As soon as she heard this, she got up quickly and went to Him. [30] Jesus had not yet come into the village but was still in the place where Martha had met Him. [31] The Jews who were with her in the house consoling her saw that Mary got up quickly and went out. So they followed her, supposing that she was going to the tomb to cry there.

[32] When Mary came to where Jesus was and saw Him, she fell at His feet and told Him, "Lord, if You had been here, my brother would not have died!"

[33] When Jesus saw her crying, and the Jews who had come with her crying, He was angry[a] in His spirit and deeply moved. [34] "Where have you put him?" He asked.

"Lord," they told Him, "come and see."

[35] Jesus wept.

[36] So the Jews said, "See how He loved him!" [37] But some of them said, "Couldn't He who opened the blind man's eyes also have kept this man from dying?"

The Seventh Sign: Raising Lazarus from the Dead

[38] Then Jesus, angry in Himself again, came to the tomb. It was a cave, and a stone was lying against it. [39] "Remove the stone," Jesus said.

Martha, the dead man's sister, told Him, "Lord, he already stinks. It's been four days."

[40] Jesus said to her, "Didn't I tell you that if you believed you would see the glory of God?"

[41] So they removed the stone. Then Jesus raised His eyes and said, "Father, I thank You that You heard Me. [42] I know that You always hear Me, but because of the crowd standing here I said this, so they may believe You sent Me." [43] After He said this, He shouted with a loud voice, "Lazarus, come out!" [44] The dead man came out bound hand and foot with linen strips and with his face wrapped in a cloth. Jesus said to them, "Loose him and let him go."

The Plot to Kill Jesus

[45] Therefore many of the Jews who came to Mary and saw what He did believed in Him. [46] But some of them went to the Pharisees and told them what Jesus had done.

[47] So the chief priests and the Pharisees convened the Sanhedrin and said, "What are we going to do since this man does many signs? [48] If we let Him continue in this way, everybody will believe in Him! Then the Romans will come and remove both our place[b] and our nation."

[49] One of them, Caiaphas, who was high priest that year, said to them, "You know nothing at all! [50] You're not considering that it is to your[c] advantage that one man should die for the people rather than the whole nation perish." [51] He did not say this on his own, but being high priest that year he prophesied that Jesus was going to die for the nation, [52] and not for the nation only, but also to unite the scattered children of God. [53] So from that day on they plotted to kill Him. [54] Therefore Jesus no longer walked openly among the Jews but departed from there to the countryside near the wilderness, to a

---

[a]11:33 The Gk word is very strong and probably indicates Jesus' anger against sin's tyranny and death. [b]11:48 The temple or possibly all of Jerusalem [c]11:50 Other mss read *to our*

11:43-44 It is often argued that the other Gospels could scarcely have left out this greatest of all Jesus' miracles if it really happened. But they do record two other resurrections Jesus performed (Mk 5:21-42; Lk 7:11-17), and by choosing to omit all but Jesus' final journey to Jerusalem, they have no place in their outline for other events in and around the holy city.

11:51-52 It is unlikely that John would view Caiaphas as a true prophet. Rather, he was referring to the Jewish tradition that high priests could prophesy and was

pointing out (ironically) how Caiaphas spoke better than he knew. Caiaphas only wanted to protect his people from the Romans; Jesus' death would actually make possible the forgiveness of anyone's sins.

11:53 Does this contradict the claim in the other Gospels that Jesus' cleansing of the temple was the reason the authorities finally decided to take His life (Mk 12:12)? No, because both John and the other Gospels recognize a series of events that eventually sealed Jesus' fate (Mk 3:6; Jn 5:18; 7:32; 8:59; 10:31).

Is There Evidence for Life After Death?

by Hank Hanegraaff

Philosophical naturalists (including most evolutionists) believe that death is the cessation of being. In their view, humans are merely bodies and brains. Though they reject metaphysical realities such as the soul, there are convincing reasons to believe that humans have an immaterial aspect to their being that transcends the material and thus can continue to exist after death.

From a legal perspective, if human beings were merely material, they could not be held accountable this year for a crime committed last year, because physical identity changes over time. We are not the same people today that we were yesterday. Every day we lose millions of microscopic particles. In fact, every seven years or so, virtually every part of our material anatomy changes, apart from aspects of our neurological system. Therefore, from a purely material perspective, the person who previously committed a crime is presently not the same person. Yet a criminal who attempts to use this line of reasoning as a defense would not get very far. Such legal maneuvering simply does not fly even in an age of scientific enlightenment. Legally and intuitively, we recognize a sameness of soul that establishes personal identity over time.

Finally, freedom of the will presupposes that we are more than material robots. If I am merely material, my choices are a function of such factors as genetic makeup and brain chemistry. Therefore, my decisions are not free; they are fatalistically determined. The implications of such a notion are profound. In a worldview that embraces fatalistic determinism, I cannot be held morally accountable for my actions, since reward and punishment make sense only if we have freedom of the will. In a solely material world, reason itself is reduced to the status of a conditioned reflex. Moreover, the very concept of love is rendered meaningless. Rather than being an act of the will, love is relegated to a robotic procedure that is fatalistically determined by physical processes.

While the legal and freedom arguments are convincing in and of themselves, there is an even more powerful and persuasive argument demonstrating the reality of life beyond the grave. That argument flows from the resurrection of Jesus Christ. The best minds of ancient and modern times have demonstrated beyond the shadow of a doubt that Christ's physical trauma was fatal; that the empty tomb is one of the best-attested facts of ancient history; that Christ's followers experienced on several occasions tangible post-resurrection appearances of Christ; and that within weeks of the resurrection, not just one, but an entire community of at least 3,000 Jews experienced such an incredible transformation that they willingly gave up sociological and theological traditions that had given them their national identity.

Through the resurrection, Christ not only demonstrated that He does not stand in a line of peers with Abraham, Buddha, or Confucius but also provided compelling evidence for life after death.

town called Ephraim. And He stayed there with the disciples.

[55] The Jewish Passover was near, and many went up to Jerusalem from the country to purify[a] themselves before the Passover. [56] They were looking for Jesus and asking one another as they stood in the temple complex: "What do you think? He won't come to the festival, will He?" [57] The chief priests and the Pharisees had given orders that if anyone knew where He was, he should report it so they could arrest Him.

The Anointing at Bethany

12 Six days before the Passover, Jesus came to Bethany where Lazarus[b] was, the one Jesus had raised from the dead. [2] So they gave a dinner for Him there; Martha was serving them, and Lazarus was one of those reclining at the table with Him. [3] Then Mary took a pound of fragrant oil—pure and expensive nard—anointed Jesus' feet, and wiped His feet with her hair. So the house was filled with the fragrance of the oil.

[4] Then one of His disciples, Judas Iscariot (who was about to betray Him), said, [5] "Why wasn't this fragrant oil sold for 300 denarii[c] and given to the poor?" [6] He didn't say this because he cared about the poor but because he was a thief. He was in charge of the money-bag and would steal part of what was put in it.

[7] Jesus answered, "Leave her alone; she has kept it for the day of My burial. [8] For you always have the poor with you, but you do not always have Me."

The Decision to Kill Lazarus

[9] Then a large crowd of the Jews learned He was there. They came not only because of Jesus, but also to see Lazarus, the one He had raised from the dead. [10] Therefore the chief priests decided to also kill Lazarus, [11] because he was the reason many of the Jews were deserting them[d] and believing in Jesus.

The Triumphal Entry

[12] The next day, when the large crowd that had come to the festival heard that Jesus was coming to Jerusalem, [13] they took palm branches and went out to meet Him. They kept shouting: "*Hosanna!* **Blessed is He who comes in the name of the Lord**[e]—the King of Israel!"

[14] Jesus found a young donkey and sat on it, just as it is written: [15] **Fear no more, Daughter Zion; look! your King is coming, sitting on a donkey's colt.**[f]

[16] His disciples did not understand these things at first. However, when Jesus was glorified, then they remembered that these things had been written about Him and that they had done these things to Him. [17] Meanwhile the crowd, which had been with Him when He called Lazarus out of the tomb and raised him from the dead, continued to testify.[g] [18] This is also why the crowd met Him, because they heard He had done this sign.

[19] Then the Pharisees said to one another, "You see? You've accomplished nothing. Look—the world has gone after Him!"

---

[a] 11:55 The law of Moses required God's people to purify or cleanse themselves so they could celebrate the Passover. Jews often came to Jerusalem a week early to do this; Nm 9:4–11. [b] 12:1 Other mss read *Lazarus who died* [c] 12:5 This amount was about a year's wages for a common worker. [d] 12:11 Lit *going away* [e] 12:13 Ps 118:25–26 [f] 12:15 Zch 9:9 [g] 12:17 Other mss read *Meanwhile the crowd, which had been with Him, continued to testify that He had called Lazarus out of the tomb and raised him from the dead.*

12:1 Mark (14:3-9) and Matthew (26:6-13) seem to place this account on the last night of Jesus' life. But there is no explicit chronological connection there, so they probably relocated this passage thematically because of its message—preparation for burial. John preserved the exact chronology. Luke 7:36-50 is an entirely separate incident with some similar details.

12:3 Did the perfume cover Jesus' feet, as here, or His head (Mk 14:3)? Probably both, since anointing a body for burial required covering the entire corpse.

12:12-19 The way people acted on Palm Sunday contrasted dramatically with the crowd's clamoring for Jesus' crucifixion five days later. Some in the two crowds would have differed, but this was also the last time the onlookers thought that maybe Jesus was going to assume an earthly kingship and free His nation. When it became clear that was not His purpose, disillusionment and hostility reappeared.

Jesus Predicts His Crucifixion

[20] Now some Greeks were among those who went up to worship at the festival. [21] So they came to Philip, who was from Bethsaida in Galilee, and requested of him, "Sir, we want to see Jesus."

[22] Philip went and told Andrew; then Andrew and Philip went and told Jesus. [23] Jesus replied to them, "The hour has come for the Son of Man to be glorified.

[24] "I assure you: Unless a grain of wheat falls into the ground and dies, it remains by itself. But if it dies, it produces a large crop.[a] [25] The one who loves his life will lose it, and the one who hates his life in this world will keep it for eternal life. [26] If anyone serves Me, he must follow Me. Where I am, there My servant also will be. If anyone serves Me, the Father will honor him.

[27] "Now My soul is troubled. What should I say—Father, save Me from this hour? But that is why I came to this hour. [28] Father, glorify Your name!"[b]

Then a voice came from heaven: "I have glorified it, and I will glorify it again!"

[29] The crowd standing there heard it and said it was thunder. Others said, "An angel has spoken to Him!"

[30] Jesus responded, "This voice came, not for Me, but for you. [31] Now is the judgment of this world. Now the ruler of this world will be cast out. [32] As for Me, if I am lifted up[c] from the earth I will draw all ⌊people⌋ to Myself." [33] He said this to signify what kind of death He was about to die.

[34] Then the crowd replied to Him, "We have heard from the law that the Messiah will remain forever. So how can You say, 'The Son of Man must be lifted up'?[c] Who is this Son of Man?"

[35] Jesus answered, "The light will be with you only a little longer. Walk while you have the light so that darkness doesn't overtake you. The one who walks in darkness doesn't know where he's going. [36] While you have the light, believe in the light so that you may become sons of light." Jesus said this, then went away and hid from them.

Isaiah's Prophecies Fulfilled

[37] Even though He had performed so many signs in their presence, they did not believe in Him. [38] But this was to fulfill the word of Isaiah the prophet, who said:[d]

> **Lord, who has believed our message?**
> **And who has the arm of the Lord been**
> **revealed to?**[e]

[39] This is why they were unable to believe, because Isaiah also said:

> [40] **He has blinded their eyes**
> **and hardened their hearts,**
> **so that they would not see**
> **with their eyes**
> **or understand with their hearts,**
> **and be converted,**
> **and I would heal them.**[f]

[41] Isaiah said these things because[g] he saw His glory and spoke about Him.

---

[a]12:24 Lit *produces much fruit*   [b]12:28 Other mss read *Your Son*   [c]12:32,34 Or *exalted*   [d]12:38 Lit *which he said*   [e]12:38 Is 53:1   [f]12:40 Is 6:10
[g]12:41 Other mss read *when*

12:27-28 These verses sound like an equivalent to Gethsemane reported in Mt, Mk, and Lk. But here the context is public, so this must have been a separate, earlier incident. If Jesus really did believe He was to be crucified (v. 32), He surely would have wrestled with that fact more than once.

12:32 This is not universalism (saving everyone) but the gospel offer to all without distinction—drawing people of every kind to Himself. Some will not receive Jesus, but for all who do, they will have the right to be children of God (1:12).

12:39-40 Is this deterministic predestination? No, for in Is 6 (quoted here) God was responding to prolonged unbelief and rebellion by Israel and still held out hope for a righteous remnant who repented (v. 13). The same was true here, as some did in fact believe (v. 42). For those who didn't, God merely confirmed their freely chosen disobedience.

12:41 In context, Is 6:10 wasn't even a prediction, much less one about Jesus. But Jews recognized typological as well as predictive prophecy. Typology is the repetition of a significant pattern of God's activity in redemptive history that can properly be ascribed only to Him. Isaiah did make predictions about the Messiah on numerous occasions, and the context of Is 6 looked

More Evidence for Life After Death

by J. P. Moreland

The case for life after death consists in empirical (observable) and nonempirical (theoretical) arguments. The empirical arguments are two: near-death experiences (NDEs) and the resurrection of Jesus. A sufficient body of evidence exists for the view that people have died, left their bodies, had various experiences, and returned to their bodies. Attempts to explain NDEs as natural phenomena fail in those cases where the disembodied person gained knowledge about things miles away (e.g., conversations of family members). One must be cautious about theological interpretations of NDEs, but their reality is well established. Some argue that, even if true, NDEs provide evidence only for temporary existence beyond death. Strictly speaking, this is correct. However, if biological death does not bring the cessation of consciousness, it is hard to see what could do so after death.

Jesus' resurrection is defended in other articles in this Bible. Suffice it to say here that if Jesus rose from the dead, this qualifies Him to speak about life after death because His resurrection provides evidence that He was the Son of God and means that He returned from the afterlife and told us about it.

The nonempirical arguments divide into theistic-dependent and theistic-independent ones. The former assume the existence of God and from that fact argue for immortality. If God is who He says He is, the case is proven beyond reasonable doubt. Three such theistic-dependent arguments are especially important.

The first is two-pronged and argues from the image and love of God. Given that humans have tremendous value as image bearers and God is a preserver of tremendously high value, then God is a preserver of persons. Moreover, given that God loves His image bearers and has a project of bringing them to full maturity and fellowship with Him, God will sustain humans to continue this love affair and His important project on their behalf.

The second argument, based on divine justice, asserts that in this life goods and evils are not evenly distributed. A just God must balance the scales in another life, and an afterlife is thus required.

Finally, there is the argument from biblical revelation. It can be established that the Bible is the truthful Word of God, and it affirms life after death. For this to be an argument, rational considerations must be marshaled on behalf of the Bible's divine status.

Two nontheistic dependent arguments exist for immortality. The first is a three-part argument from desire: (1) The desire for life after death is a natural desire. (2) Every natural desire corresponds to some real state of affairs that can fulfill it. (3) Therefore, the desire for life after death corresponds to some real state of affairs—namely life after death—that fulfills it.

Critics claim that the desire for immortality is nothing but an expression of ethical egoism. People do not universally desire it, and even when they do, it is a learned, not a natural, desire. Further, even if it is a natural desire, sometimes such desires are frustrated. Thus the desire argument is not necessarily a strong argument, but nonetheless it does have some merit.

The second argument claims that consciousness and the self are immaterial, not physical, and this supports belief in life after death in two ways: (1) It makes disembodied existence and personal identity in the afterlife intelligible. (2) It provides evidence for the existence of God. This, in turn, provides grounds for reintroducing the theistic-dependent arguments for life after death.

The argument for consciousness being nonphysical involves the claim that once one gets an accurate description of consciousness—sensations, emotions, thoughts, beliefs—it becomes clear that it is not physical. Conscious states are characterized by their inner, private, qualitative feel made known by introspection. Since physical states lack these features, consciousness is not physical.

The case for an immaterial self is rooted in the claim that in first-person introspection we are aware of our own egos as immaterial centers of consciousness. This awareness grounds intuitions that when one has an arm cut off, has a portion of one's brain removed, or gains or loses memories and personality traits, one does not become a partial person or a different person altogether.

While these two arguments provide some grounds for belief in an afterlife, they are far from conclusive. At the end of the day, the justification of belief in life after death is largely theistic dependent.

[42] Nevertheless, many did believe in Him even among the rulers, but because of the Pharisees they did not confess Him, so they would not be banned from the synagogue. [43] For they loved praise from men more than praise from God. [a]

A Summary of Jesus' Mission

[44] Then Jesus cried out, "The one who believes in Me believes not in Me, but in Him who sent Me. [45] And the one who sees Me sees Him who sent Me. [46] I have come as a light into the world, so that everyone who believes in Me would not remain in darkness. [47] If anyone hears My words and doesn't keep them, I do not judge him; for I did not come to judge the world but to save the world. [48] The one who rejects Me and doesn't accept My sayings has this as his judge: [b] the word I have spoken will judge him on the last day. [49] For I have not spoken on My own, but the Father Himself who sent Me has given Me a command as to what I should say and what I should speak. [50] I know that His command is eternal life. So the things that I speak, I speak just as the Father has told Me."

Jesus Washes His Disciples' Feet

13 Before the Passover Festival, Jesus knew that His hour had come to depart from this world to the Father. Having loved His own who were in the world, He loved them to the end. [c]

[2] Now by the time of supper, the Devil had already put it into the heart of Judas, Simon Iscariot's son, to betray Him. [3] Jesus knew

[a]12:43 Lit *loved glory of men more than glory of God; v. 41; Jn 5:41*   [b]12:48 Lit *has the one judging him*   [c]13:1 *to the end = completely* or *always*

beyond the present, evil generation of Isaiah, so it is understandable why John would believe that Isaiah previewed Jesus' glory.

13:1 If it was just before the Passover feast in verse 1, did John intend for the meal of verse 2 to be a different one from the Passover? Probably not. Verse 1 is a small paragraph that functions as a headline over all of chapters 13–17. Verse 2 then describes the very Passover meal that had just been mentioned. Not only did various details match the accounts from the other Gospels that are more clearly based on Passover, but only

on that night would anyone have imagined that Judas was leaving to give something for the poor (v. 29). The feast lasted for a week, so he could also have needed to buy more provisions (v. 29).

13:2-17 Only John describes the foot washing; only the other Gospels present Jesus' words over the bread and the cup. But both fit neatly together as part of the same meal, a Jewish Passover feast, which Jesus reinterpreted as symbolizing His upcoming, self-giving death for the sins of humanity.

that the Father had given everything into His hands, that He had come from God, and that He was going back to God. *4* So He got up from supper, laid aside His robe, took a towel, and tied it around Himself. *5* Next, He poured water into a basin and began to wash His disciples' feet and to dry them with the towel tied around Him.

6 He came to Simon Peter, who asked Him, "Lord, are You going to wash my feet?"

7 Jesus answered him, "What I'm doing you don't understand now, but afterwards you will know."

8 "You will never wash my feet—ever!" Peter said.

Jesus replied, "If I don't wash you, you have no part with Me."

9 Simon Peter said to Him, "Lord, not only my feet, but also my hands and my head."

10 "One who has bathed," Jesus told him, "doesn't need to wash anything except his feet, but he is completely clean. You are clean, but not all of you." *11* For He knew who would betray Him. This is why He said, "You are not all clean."

The Meaning of Footwashing

12 When Jesus had washed their feet and put on His robe, He reclined[a] again and said to them, "Do you know what I have done for you? *13* You call Me Teacher and Lord. This is well said, for I am. *14* So if I, your Lord and Teacher, have washed your feet, you also ought to wash one another's feet. *15* For I have given you an example that you also should do just as I have done for you.

16 "I assure you: A slave is not greater than his master,[b] and a messenger is not greater than the one who sent him. *17* If you know these things, you are blessed if you do them.

18 I'm not speaking about all of you; I know those I have chosen. But the Scripture must be fulfilled: **The one who eats My bread**[c] **has raised his heel against Me.**[d]

19 "I am telling you now before it happens, so that when it does happen you will believe that I am ⌊He⌋. *20* I assure you: The one who receives whomever I send receives Me, and the one who receives Me receives Him who sent Me."

Judas' Betrayal Predicted

21 When Jesus had said this, He was troubled in His spirit and testified, "I assure you: One of you will betray Me!"

22 The disciples started looking at one another—uncertain which one He was speaking about. *23* One of His disciples, the one Jesus loved, was reclining close beside Jesus.[e] *24* Simon Peter motioned to him to find out who it was He was talking about. *25* So he leaned back against Jesus and asked Him, "Lord, who is it?"

26 Jesus replied, "He's the one I give the piece of bread to after I have dipped it." When He had dipped the bread, He gave it to Judas, Simon Iscariot's son.[f] *27* After ⌊Judas ate⌋ the piece of bread, Satan entered him. Therefore Jesus told him, "What you're doing, do quickly."

28 None of those reclining at the table knew why He told him this. *29* Since Judas kept the money-bag, some thought that Jesus was telling him, "Buy what we need for the festival," or that he should give something to the poor. *30* After receiving the piece of bread, he went out immediately. And it was night.

The New Commandment

31 When he had gone out, Jesus said, "Now the Son of Man is glorified, and God is glo-

a13:12 At important meals the custom was to recline on a mat at a low table and lean on the left elbow.   b13:16 Or *lord*   c13:18 Other mss read *eats bread with Me*   d13:18 Ps 41:9   e13:23 Lit *reclining at Jesus' breast;* that is, on His right; Jn 1:18   f13:26 Other mss read *Judas Iscariot, Simon's son*

13:16 In other contexts, servants can become greater than their masters. But this is not true with Jesus and His followers, especially when the issues are those of menial service or persecution, which naturally we wish we could avoid (15:20).

13:18-30 Jesus would have shared His bread with all of the Twelve, so verse 18 means merely that one of His most intimate followers would betray Him. Verses 23-26 describe what probably were whispered remarks among those seated closest to Jesus. Jesus' words in verse 27 may then have been spoken loudly enough for all to hear—but not to understand.

rified in Him. [32] If God is glorified in Him,[a] God will also glorify Him in Himself and will glorify Him at once.

[33] "Children, I am with you a little while longer. You will look for Me, and just as I told the Jews, 'Where I am going you cannot come,' so now I tell you.

[34] "I give you a new commandment: love one another. Just as I have loved you, you must also love one another. [35] By this all people will know that you are My disciples, if you have love for one another."

Peter's Denials Predicted

[36] "Lord," Simon Peter said to Him, "where are You going?"

Jesus answered, "Where I am going you cannot follow Me now, but you will follow later."

[37] "Lord," Peter asked, "why can't I follow You now? I will lay down my life for You!"

[38] Jesus replied, "Will you lay down your life for Me? I assure you: A rooster will not crow until you have denied Me three times.

The Way to the Father

14 "Your heart must not be troubled. Believe[b] in God; believe also in Me. [2] In My Father's house are many dwelling places;[c] if not, I would have told you. I am going away to prepare a place for you. [3] If I go away and prepare a place for you, I will come back and receive you to Myself, so that where I am you may be also. [4] You know the way where I am going."[d]

[5] "Lord," Thomas said, "we don't know where You're going. How can we know the way?"

[6] Jesus told him, "I am the way, the truth, and the life. No one comes to the Father except through Me.

Jesus Reveals the Father

[7] "If you know Me, you will also know[e] My Father. From now on you do know Him and have seen Him."

[8] "Lord," said Philip, "show us the Father, and that's enough for us."

[9] Jesus said to him, "Have I been among you all this time without your knowing Me, Philip? The one who has seen Me has seen the Father. How can you say, 'Show us the Father'? [10] Don't you believe that I am in the Father and the Father is in Me? The words I speak to you I do not speak on My own. The Father who lives in Me does His works. [11] Believe Me that I am in the Father and the Father is in Me. Otherwise, believe[f] because of the works themselves.

Praying in Jesus' Name

[12] "I assure you: The one who believes in Me will also do the works that I do. And he will do even greater works than these, because I am going to the Father. [13] Whatever you ask in My name, I will do it so that the Father may be glorified in the Son. [14] If you ask Me[g] anything in My name, I will do it.[h]

---

[a]13:32 Other mss omit *If God is glorified in Him* [b]14:1 Or *You believe* [c]14:2 The Vg used the Lat term *mansio*, a traveler's resting place. The Gk word is related to the verb *meno*, meaning *remain* or *stay*, which occurs 40 times in John. [d]14:4 Other mss read this verse: *And you know where I am going, and you know the way* [e]14:7 Other mss read *If you had known Me, you would have known* [f]14:11 Other mss read *believe Me* [g]14:14 Other mss omit *Me* [h]14:14 Other mss omit all of v. 14

14:6 Can we really believe that all those who have never even heard of Jesus are lost? This is a question to which orthodox Christians have given several different answers throughout history. However, this verse does not directly answer it. At the very least John affirmed that, if God forgives anyone, it will be because of Christ's atoning work on the cross. As for whether people have to have heard of Jesus for God to apply the benefits of Christ's death to them, that will have to be decided on the basis of other texts and themes.

14:9-11 Two errors are guarded against here. Verse 9 by itself could suggest that the Son is the Father incar-

nate, that there are no distinctions between the two persons. But verses 10-11 make it clear that is not the case. These verses also guard against fully separating the Father and the Son into distinct gods. Each interpenetrates the other—what the ancient Greeks called *perichoresis*.

14:14; 15:16; 16:23 These are not "blank checks"—promises to supply everything anyone requests. "In My name" corresponds to "according to My character" and thus is parallel to other texts that require us to leave room for God's will to overrule ours (e.g., Mt 6:10; Jms 4:15).

How Does the Bible Relate to Islam?

by Barbara B. Pemberton

*I*slam teaches that throughout history God has sent prophets, from Adam to Noah to Jesus and ultimately Muhammad, all with the same message: There is only one God, who desires people to pursue good and to prevent evil. Christians and Jews, "People of the Book," are believed to be the remaining followers of earlier divine, but corrupted, revelations. Islam's scripture, the Qur'an, is understood by Muslims to have restored God's original guidance. The Qur'an includes numerous biblical personalities but recognizes as authentic only three sections of biblical literature: the Torah of Moses, the Evangel of Jesus, and the Psalms of David.

Muslims see many of their beliefs and practices as biblical: the existence of only one God, the prophets, heaven, hell, angels, and a day of judgment. They also see the importance of charity, prayer, and fasting in the Bible. Although Muslims believe that Jesus was only a prophet and not divine, they do believe the accounts of His virgin birth, sinless nature, miracles, and second coming.

The Qur'an accuses Jews and Christians of distorting their earlier revelation by deliberately suppressing the truth or by false interpretation. Muslims charge that the OT and NT contain logical inconsistencies, improbabilities, and factual errors. Charges against the OT include false reports of immorality (David and Bathsheba), missing doctrines (afterlife in the Torah), and incompatibility with science. The Evangel has been corrupted with inaccurate historical references, discrepancies in the Gospel accounts, and fabrications (such as the crucifixion). Christians and Jews allegedly suppressed or removed biblical predictions of Muhammad. For example, Psalm 84:4-6 is said to be about Muhammad, who overcame his childhood disadvantages by God's grace. Jesus supposedly predicted the coming Prophet Muhammad when He spoke of the "Counselor" in John 14.

Islam rejects the concept of human participation in the process of revelation that shows in the varieties of biblical books (Gospels, Letters, etc.). Jesus' original message is deemed lost. Muslims believe that Gospel authors, writing long after Jesus, altered the message to promote their own points of view. Paul's letters are supposed to promote a "mystical" Christ and "false" doctrines such as the resurrection. Another Muslim argument against biblical reliability is the lack of a record that the original texts passed from one generation to the next.

Muslims are, of course, correct that the Bible is older than the Qur'an. But there is not a shred of evidence the Bible has been corrupted. Indeed, the transmission of its text is by far the most accurate of any from the ancient world (see "Has the Bible Been Accurately Copied Down Through the Centuries?" p. 468). The Bible is not compromised by God using human personalities in its writing any more than when He uses human personality in the spoken word of prophets. Moreover, powerful evidence supports, among other things, the historicity of Jesus' crucifixion and resurrection (see "Did Jesus Really Rise from the Dead?" p. 1728). Prayerful Christians can help to correct Muslim misconceptions about the Bible (e.g., by showing that the Bible does not sanction the sinfulness of Western culture). Indeed, Christ's followers should befriend Muslims so the Holy Spirit can bring conviction to their hearts through the powerful Word of God (Heb 4:12).

Another Counselor Promised

[15] "If you love Me, you will keep[a] My commandments. [16] And I will ask the Father, and He will give you another Counselor to be with you forever. [17] He is the Spirit of truth. The world is unable to receive Him because it doesn't see Him or know Him. But you do know Him, because He remains with you and will be[b] in you. [18] I will not leave you as orphans; I am coming to you.

The Father, the Son, and the Holy Spirit

[19] "In a little while the world will see Me no longer, but you will see Me. Because I live, you will live too. [20] In that day you will know that I am in My Father, you are in Me, and I am in you. [21] The one who has My commands and keeps them is the one who loves Me. And the one who loves Me will be loved by My Father. I also will love him and will reveal Myself to him."

[22] Judas (not Iscariot) said to Him, "Lord, how is it You're going to reveal Yourself to us and not to the world?"

[23] Jesus answered, "If anyone loves Me, he will keep My word. My Father will love him, and We will come to him and make Our home with him. [24] The one who doesn't love Me will not keep My words. The word that you hear is not Mine but is from the Father who sent Me.

[25] "I have spoken these things to you while I remain with you. [26] But the Counselor, the Holy Spirit—the Father will send Him in My name—will teach you all things and remind you of everything I have told you.

Jesus' Gift of Peace

[27] "Peace I leave with you. My peace I give to you. I do not give to you as the world gives. Your heart must not be troubled or fearful. [28] You have heard Me tell you, 'I am going away and I am coming to you.' If you loved Me, you would have rejoiced that I am going to the Father, because the Father is greater than I. [29] I have told you now before it happens so that when it does happen you may believe. [30] I will not talk with you much longer, because the ruler of the world is coming. He has no power over Me.[c] [31] On the contrary, ₍I am going away₎[d] so that the world may know that I love the Father. Just as the Father commanded Me, so I do.

"Get up; let's leave this place.

The Vine and the Branches

15 "I am the true vine, and My Father is the vineyard keeper. [2] Every branch in Me that does not produce fruit He removes, and He prunes every branch that produces fruit so that it will produce more fruit. [3] You are already clean because of the word I have spoken to you. [4] Remain in Me, and I in you. Just as a branch is unable to produce fruit by itself unless it remains on the vine, so neither can you unless you remain in Me.

---

[a]14:15 Other mss read *If you love Me, keep* (as a command) [b]14:17 Other mss read *and is* [c]14:30 Lit *He has nothing in Me* [d]14:31 Probably refers to the cross

14:26; 15:26-27; 16:13 Two themes are balanced in these texts. The Spirit would lead the disciples into further truth after Jesus was gone, but it would be based on what they already knew about Him and had learned from Him. Denying that the Spirit can still give believers the gift of prophecy is unwarranted, but allegations of such prophecies must always be tested and can never contradict, or be elevated to the same level as, Scripture (see 1 Co 14:29-33).

14:28 This is a clear statement of Jesus' functional subordination to the Father described in the note on 5:16-30. It does not deny the simultaneous essential equality of Father and Son.

14:31 Jesus seems to have been ready to leave the upper room but continued talking for another three chapters. Many see an editorially imposed unity of different sources here, but it may be better to see chapters 15–17 as having been spoken after the group had left the house and was headed for the garden. They would have passed vineyards en route, along with the temple and its golden carving of a vine on it, perhaps inspiring 15:1-8. After all, 18:1 doesn't say they left "the house," just that they "went out." In fact, it sounds like they were already on the edge of the Kidron Valley beneath the temple.

15:2-8 Do verses 2 and 6 deny John's promise that God will protect those who are truly His (6:39; 10:29)? No, but they are reminders that true believers will persevere (v. 4; see note on 8:30-31). Those who don't persevere show that they were never truly Christ's (1 Jn 2:19).

[5] "I am the vine; you are the branches. The one who remains in Me and I in him produces much fruit, because you can do nothing without Me. [6] If anyone does not remain in Me, he is thrown aside like a branch and he withers. They gather them, throw them into the fire, and they are burned. [7] If you remain in Me and My words remain in you, ask whatever you want and it will be done for you. [8] My Father is glorified by this: that you produce much fruit and prove to be[a] My disciples.

Christlike Love

[9] "As the Father has loved Me, I have also loved you. Remain in My love. [10] If you keep My commands you will remain in My love, just as I have kept My Father's commands and remain in His love.

[11] "I have spoken these things to you so that My joy may be in you and your joy may be complete. [12] This is My command: love one another as I have loved you. [13] No one has greater love than this, that someone would lay down his life for his friends. [14] You are My friends if you do what I command you. [15] I do not call you slaves anymore, because a slave doesn't know what his master[b] is doing. I have called you friends, because I have made known to you everything I have heard from My Father. [16] You did not choose Me, but I chose you. I appointed you that you should go out and produce fruit and that your fruit should remain, so that whatever you ask the Father in My name, He will give you. [17] This is what I command you: love one another.

Persecutions Predicted

[18] "If the world hates you, understand that it hated Me before it hated you. [19] If you were of the world, the world would love ⌊you as⌋ its own. However, because you are not of the world, but I have chosen you out of it, the world hates you. [20] Remember the word I spoke to you: 'A slave is not greater than his master.' If they persecuted Me, they will also persecute you. If they kept My word, they will also keep yours. [21] But they will do all these things to you on account of My name, because they don't know the One who sent Me. [22] If I had not come and spoken to them, they would not have sin.[c] Now they have no excuse for their sin. [23] The one who hates Me also hates My Father. [24] If I had not done the works among them that no one else has done, they would not have sin. Now they have seen and hated both Me and My Father. [25] But ⌊this happened⌋ so that the statement written in their law might be fulfilled: **They hated Me for no reason.**[d]

Coming Testimony and Rejection

[26] "When the Counselor comes, the One I will send to you from the Father—the Spirit of truth who proceeds from the Father—He will testify about Me. [27] You also will testify, because you have been with Me from the beginning.

16 "I have told you these things to keep you from stumbling. [2] They will ban you from the synagogues. In fact, a time is coming when anyone who kills you will think he is offering service to God. [3] They will do these things because they haven't known the Father or Me. [4] But I have told you these things so that when their time[e] comes you may remember I told them to you. I didn't tell you these things from the beginning, because I was with you.

The Counselor's Ministry

[5] "But now I am going away to Him who sent Me, and not one of you asks Me, 'Where

---

[a]15:8 Or *and become*   [b]15:15 Or *lord*   [c]15:22 To *have sin* is an idiom that refers to guilt caused by sin.   [d]15:25 Ps 69:4   [e]16:4 Other mss read *when the time*

15:22,24 There are different kinds of guilt. Unwitting sins can be excused more readily than intentional ones. All people sin and are guilty in God's eyes as a result, but not all are held equally accountable (Lk 12:47-48; Rm 5:13-14).

16:5 How could Jesus say no one was asking Him where He was going when that was precisely Thomas's question in 14:5? Probably the focus is on the present tense. No one was asking right now, and they should have been, since they still didn't understand. This solution

are You going?' [6] Yet, because I have spoken these things to you, sorrow has filled your heart. [7] Nevertheless, I am telling you the truth. It is for your benefit that I go away, because if I don't go away the Counselor will not come to you. If I go, I will send Him to you. [8] When He comes, He will convict the world about sin, righteousness, and judgment: [9] about sin, because they do not believe in Me; [10] about righteousness, because I am going to the Father and you will no longer see Me; [11] and about judgment, because the ruler of this world has been judged.

[12] "I still have many things to tell you, but you can't bear them now. [13] When the Spirit of truth comes, He will guide you into all the truth. For He will not speak on His own, but He will speak whatever He hears. He will also declare to you what is to come. [14] He will glorify Me, because He will take from what is Mine and declare it to you. [15] Everything the Father has is Mine. This is why I told you that He takes from what is Mine and will declare it to you.

Sorrow Turned to Joy

[16] "A little while and you will no longer see Me; again a little while and you will see Me." [a]

[17] Therefore some of His disciples said to one another, "What is this He tells us: 'A little while and you will not see Me; again a little while and you will see Me'; and, 'because I am going to the Father'?" [18] They said, "What is this He is saying, [b] 'A little while'? We don't know what He's talking about!"

[19] Jesus knew they wanted to question Him, so He said to them, "Are you asking one another about what I said, 'A little while and you will not see Me; again a little while and you will see Me'?

[20] "I assure you: You will weep and wail, but the world will rejoice. You will become sorrowful, but your sorrow will turn to joy. [21] When a woman is in labor she has pain because her time has come. But when she has given birth to a child, she no longer remembers the suffering because of the joy that a person has been born into the world. [22] So you also have sorrow [c] now. But I will see you again. Your hearts will rejoice, and no one will rob you of your joy. [23] In that day you will not ask Me anything.

"I assure you: Anything you ask the Father in My name, He will give you. [24] Until now you have asked for nothing in My name. Ask and you will receive, that your joy may be complete.

Jesus the Victor

[25] "I have spoken these things to you in figures of speech. A time is coming when I will no longer speak to you in figures, but I will tell you plainly about the Father. [26] In that day you will ask in My name. I am not telling you that I will make requests to the Father on your behalf. [27] For the Father Himself loves you, because you have loved Me and have believed that I came from God. [d] [28] I came from the Father and have come into the world. Again, I am leaving the world and going to the Father."

[29] "Ah!" His disciples said. "Now You're speaking plainly and not using any figurative language. [30] Now we know that You know everything and don't need anyone to question

---

[a]16:16 Other mss add *because I am going to the Father*   [b]16:18 Other mss omit *He is saying*   [c]16:22 Other mss read *will have sorrow*
[d]16:27 Other mss read *from the Father*

---

is made plausible by the fact that the disciples, whose questions had punctuated the narrative throughout 13:36–14:22, had fallen silent since then.

16:24 Obviously, the disciples had asked Jesus about and for many things, but here He was referring to arrangements after His death and resurrection. Then, since He would be physically absent, they would ask God "in My name"—that is, through Jesus' power and in keeping with His character. This was even less a blank check

than 14:14, 15:16, and 16:23, since Jesus did not specify what God would grant in response to their asking, merely that they would "receive."

16:29-31 Finally the disciples claimed to understand. But verse 31 is either an ironic exclamation or a question, implying that they really still hadn't caught on. They were going to abandon Jesus in the garden that very night (v. 32). Only after the resurrection would they fully understand.

You. By this we believe that You came from God."

³¹ Jesus responded to them, "Do you now believe? ³² Look: An hour is coming, and has come, when each of you will be scattered to his own home, and you will leave Me alone. Yet I am not alone, because the Father is with Me. ³³ I have told you these things so that in Me you may have peace. You will have suffering in this world. Be courageous! I have conquered the world."

Jesus Prays for Himself

17 Jesus spoke these things, looked up to heaven, and said:

Father,
the hour has come.
Glorify Your Son
so that the Son may glorify You,
² for You gave Him authority
over all flesh;ᵃ
so He may give eternal life
to all You have given Him.
³ This is eternal life:
that they may know You,
the only true God,
and the One You have sent—
Jesus Christ.
⁴ I have glorified You on the earth
by completing the work You gave Me
to do.
⁵ Now, Father, glorify Me
in Your presence

with that glory I had with You
before the world existed.

Jesus Prays for His Disciples

⁶ I have revealed Your name
to the men You gave Me
from the world.
They were Yours, You gave them to Me,
and they have kept Your word.
⁷ Now they know that all things
You have given to Me are from You,
⁸ because the words that You gave Me,
I have given them.
They have received them
and have known for certain
that I came from You.
They have believed that You sent Me.
⁹ I prayᵇ for them.
I am not praying for the world
but for those You have given Me,
because they are Yours.
¹⁰ All My things are Yours,
and Yours are Mine,
and I have been glorified in them.
¹¹ I am no longer in the world,
but they are in the world,
and I am coming to You.
Holy Father,
protectᶜ them by Your name
that You have given Me,
so that they may be one as We are one.
¹² While I was with them,
I was protecting them by Your name
that You have given Me.

ᵃ17:2 Or *people* ᵇ17:9 Lit *ask* (throughout this passage) ᶜ17:11 Lit *keep* (throughout this passage)

17:1-5 Isn't this the height of mutual self-serving behavior—the Father and the Son glorifying each other for eternity? There are deities in the religions of the world who behave that way, but here it is crucial to observe that what brings glory to the Godhead is the opportunity of eternal life for anyone who believes (v. 2)—an opportunity no other religion provides.

17:7-8 Did they really know so much and "for certain"? This verse does not deny the many things the disciples still did not understand. But compared to those who had not followed Jesus, it is true that they had "received" His "words." The original text of "with certainty" can also be translated "truly."

17:9 That Jesus was not praying for the world on this specific occasion does not mean that He never prayed

for fallen humanity or that we shouldn't pray for them either. Indeed, He was praying for those who would come to faith through the apostles' message, that their unity would be a sign to a lost world that would watch what they do (v. 23).

17:12 Judas was not an exception to the principle that Jesus would lose none of those God gave Him (6:39; 10:29), for he was doomed from the outset—never truly one of Christ's followers (6:70-71). Yet even here predestination never overrides free will and human accountability (Mk 14:20-21). No one Scripture is specifically mentioned, though there are echoes of Ps 41:9 and 109:4-13. If Judas had chosen not to betray Jesus, someone else likely would have stepped forward.

I guarded them and not one of them
  is lost,
except the son of destruction,[a]
so that the Scripture may be fulfilled.
[13] Now I am coming to You,
  and I speak these things in the world
  so that they may have My joy completed
    in them.
[14] I have given them Your word.
  The world hated them
  because they are not of the world,
  as I am not of the world.
[15] I am not praying
  that You take them out of the world
  but that You protect them
    from the evil one.
[16] They are not of the world,
  as I am not of the world.
[17] Sanctify[b] them by the truth;
  Your word is truth.
[18] As You sent Me into the world,
  I also have sent them into the world.
[19] I sanctify Myself for them,
  so they also may be sanctified
    by the truth.

Jesus Prays for All Believers

[20] I pray not only for these,
  but also for those who believe in Me
  through their message.
[21] May they all be one,
  as You, Father, are in Me and I am
    in You.
  May they also be one[c] in Us,
  so the world may believe
    You sent Me.
[22] I have given them the glory
  You have given Me.
  May they be one as We are one.

[23] I am in them and You are in Me.
  May they be made completely one,
  so the world may know You have
    sent Me
  and have loved them as
    You have loved Me.
[24] Father,
  I desire those You have given Me
  to be with Me where I am.
  Then they will see My glory,
  which You have given Me
  because You loved Me
    before the world's foundation.
[25] Righteous Father!
  The world has not known You.
  However, I have known You,
  and these have known that You sent Me.
[26] I made Your name known to them
  and will make it known,
  so the love You have loved Me with
  may be in them and I may be in them.

Jesus Betrayed

18 After Jesus had said these things, He went out with His disciples across the Kidron Valley, where there was a garden, and He and His disciples went into it. [2] Judas, who betrayed Him, also knew the place, because Jesus often met there with His disciples. [3] So Judas took a company of soldiers and some temple police from the chief priests and the Pharisees and came there with lanterns, torches, and weapons.

[4] Then Jesus, knowing everything that was about to happen to Him, went out and said to them, "Who is it you're looking for?"

[5] "Jesus the Nazarene," they answered.

"I am He,"[d] Jesus told them.

---

[a]17:12 The one destined for destruction, loss, or perdition [b]17:17 Set apart for special use [c]17:21 Other mss omit *one* [d]18:5 Lit *I am*; see note at Jn 8:58

17:21-23 Obviously, believers cannot be one with either the Father or the Son in every way the persons of the Godhead are one with each other, for we are not God. On the other hand, the unity among Christians is more than the invisible oneness of all believers; it is something that demonstrates itself in outward, tangible, loving cooperation for powerful evangelistic purposes and results.

18:3 A "company of soldiers" would most naturally refer to Romans. But the other Gospels describe no Romans involved in the arresting party. On the other hand, it is hard to believe the Jews would undertake so strategic an arrest without approval from the Roman governor. If any fear of a mob uprising remained, the Romans would want to be involved.

Can Something Be True for You and Not for Me?

by Paul Copan

"*I*t's all relative." "That's true for you but not for me." "That's just your reality." "Who are you to impose your values on others?" The relativist believes truth functions more like opinion or perspective and that truth depends upon your culture, context, or even personal choices. Thus evil actions by Nazis or terrorists are explained away ("We don't like it, but they have their reasons"). Relativism, however, is seriously flawed.

Relativism cannot escape proclaiming a truth that corresponds to reality. "The moon is made of cheese" is false because it does not match up with the way things are, with what is the case. As Christians, we claim the biblical story is true because it conforms to the actualities of God's existence and His dealings with human beings. Truth is a relationship—a match-up with what is real or actual. An idea is false when it does not. But what of those making such claims as "Reality is like a wet lump of clay—we can shape it any way we want" (a relativistic idea known as *anti-realism*)? We can rightly call such statements into question. After all, these persons believe that their view corresponds to the way things are. If you disagree with them, they believe you are wrong. Notice, too, that they believe there is at least one thing that is not subject to human manipulation—namely, the unshakable reality that reality is like a wet lump of clay that we can shape any way we want to! So we can ask: "Is that lump-of-clay idea something you made up?" If it applies to everyone, then the statement is incoherent. If it doesn't, then it's nothing more than one's perspective. Why take it seriously? And if there's no objective truth or reality, how do we know that our beliefs are not delusional?

Relativism is self-contradictory. If someone claims to be a relativist, don't believe it. A relativist will say that your belief is true for you but his is true for him; there is no objective truth that applies to all people. The only problem is that this statement itself is an objective truth that applies to all people! (Even when he says, "That's true for you but not for me," he believes his view applies to more than just one person!) To show the self-contradictory nature of relativism, we can simply preface relativistic assertions this way: "It's objectively true that 'That's true for you but not for me'" or "It's true that 'There is no truth.'" The bold contradiction becomes apparent. Or what of the line that sincere belief makes something (Buddhism, Marxism, Christianity) true? We must ask, is this principle universal and absolute? Is it true even if I don't sincerely believe it? That is, what if I sincerely believe that sincere belief does not make something real? Both views obviously cannot be true.

The basis and conclusion of relativism are objectively true. Ask the relativist why she takes this view. She'll probably say, "So many people believe so many different things." The problem here is that she believes this to be universally true and beyond dispute. Furthermore, she believes that the logical conclusion to draw from the vast array of beliefs is that relativism must be the case. The relativist doesn't believe that all these different beliefs are a matter of personal preference. The basis for relativism (the variety of beliefs), and the conclusion that relativism obviously follows from it, turn out to be logical and objectively true—for all people, not just the relativist!

Relativism will always be selective. People usually aren't relativists about the law of gravity, drug prescription labels, or the stock index. They're usually relativists when it comes to God's existence, sexual morality, or cheating on exams. But try cutting in line in front of a relativist, helping yourself to his property, or taking a sledgehammer to his car—and you will find out that he believes his rights have been violated! Rights and relativism don't mix. But if "it's all relative," why get mad at anyone?

Relativism is usually motivated by a personal agenda—the drive for self-control. Atheist philosopher John Searle uncovers what's behind relativism: "It satisfies a basic urge to power. It just seems too disgusting, somehow, that we should have to be at the mercy of the 'real world.'" We want to be in charge. Now, pointing out one's motivation is not an argument against relativism; still, it's a noteworthy consideration. Truth often takes a backseat to freedom. But clearly, when a person shrugs off arguments for the inescapability of objective truth with "Whatever," he has another agenda in mind. Relativism makes no personal demands upon us—to love God, to be people of integrity, to help improve society. Even if relativism is false, it is convenient.

Judas, who betrayed Him, was also standing with them. ⁶ When He told them, "I am He," they stepped back and fell to the ground.

⁷ Then He asked them again, "Who is it you're looking for?"

"Jesus the Nazarene," they said.

⁸ "I told you I am ₍He₎," Jesus replied. "So if you're looking for Me, let these men go." ⁹ This was to fulfill the words He had said: "I have not lost one of those You have given Me."

¹⁰ Then Simon Peter, who had a sword, drew it, struck the high priest's slave, and cut off his right ear. (The slave's name was Malchus.)

¹¹ At that, Jesus said to Peter, "Sheathe your sword! Am I not to drink the cup the Father has given Me?"

Jesus Arrested and Taken to Annas

¹² Then the company of soldiers, the commander, and the Jewish temple police arrested Jesus and tied Him up. ¹³ First they led Him to Annas, for he was the father-in-law of Caiaphas, who was high priest that year. ¹⁴ Caiaphas was the one who had advised the Jews that it was advantageous that one man should die for the people.

Peter Denies Jesus

¹⁵ Meanwhile Simon Peter was following Jesus, as was another disciple. That disciple was an acquaintance of the high priest; so he went with Jesus into the high priest's courtyard. ¹⁶ But Peter remained standing outside by the door. So the other disciple, the one known to the high priest, went out and

18:6 It is hard to know if we are to take this as a miraculous event or not. Did Jesus' would-be attackers recoil and unwittingly bow down before Him? Or perhaps the imagery is much more mundane. Surprised by the forthrightness of Jesus' self-disclosure, some soldiers may have stumbled backward on the hillside, causing others to fall down as well.

18:12-14,19-23 John described a hearing before Annas, whereas the other Gospels set the trial before the Sanhedrin. Both are plausible, in sequence. As the prior high priest, deposed by Rome, Annas would have still been respected by the Jewish leaders, since the office was supposed to be for life. "That year" (v. 13) didn't

imply that Caiaphas was high priest only that year; it probably carried the force of "that fateful year." John knew the subsequent trial (vv. 24,28) but chose not to narrate it in detail, probably because it was already well known from the other Gospels.

18:15-18,25-27 The identities of those who accused Peter of being one of Jesus' disciples vary a little from one Gospel to the next. In the confused and frantic activity surrounding a nighttime arrest and interrogation, it would be natural for numerous people to confront Peter. But all four Gospels agree that Peter denied Christ exactly three times, even as He had predicted (13:38).

spoke to the girl who was the doorkeeper and brought Peter in.

[17] Then the slave girl who was the doorkeeper said to Peter, "You aren't one of this man's disciples too, are you?"

"I am not!" he said. [18] Now the slaves and the temple police had made a charcoal fire, because it was cold. They were standing there warming themselves, and Peter was standing with them, warming himself.

Jesus before Annas

[19] The high priest questioned Jesus about His disciples and about His teaching.

[20] "I have spoken openly to the world," Jesus answered him. "I have always taught in the synagogue and in the temple complex, where all the Jews congregate, and I haven't spoken anything in secret. [21] Why do you question Me? Question those who heard what I told them. Look, they know what I said."

[22] When He had said these things, one of the temple police standing by slapped Jesus,

TWISTED SCRIPTURE
John 18:20

Jesus offered His gospel openly and freely to all who would listen, whereas the mystery religions of His day and ours (e.g., the Rosicrucians) require that one be initiated into their group before receiving knowledge. Initiation often involves occult rites, which are hidden from public view, and the payment of fees before one can acquire the teaching that the group has to offer. The Mormons conduct secret rites in their temples, including baptism for the dead and the sealing of marriages for eternity.

saying, "Is this the way you answer the high priest?"

[23] "If I have spoken wrongly," Jesus answered him, "give evidence [a] about the wrong; but if rightly, why do you hit Me?"

[24] Then Annas sent Him bound to Caiaphas the high priest.

Peter Denies Jesus Twice More

[25] Now Simon Peter was standing and warming himself. They said to him, "You aren't one of His disciples too, are you?"

He denied it and said, "I am not!"

[26] One of the high priest's slaves, a relative of the man whose ear Peter had cut off, said, "Didn't I see you with Him in the garden?"

[27] Peter then denied it again. Immediately a rooster crowed.

Jesus before Pilate

[28] Then they took Jesus from Caiaphas to the governor's headquarters. It was early morning. They did not enter the headquarters themselves; otherwise they would be defiled and unable to eat the Passover.

[29] Then Pilate came out to them and said, "What charge do you bring against this man?"

[30] They answered him, "If this man weren't a criminal,[b] we wouldn't have handed Him over to you."

[31] So Pilate told them, "Take Him yourselves and judge Him according to your law."

"It's not legal[c] for us to put anyone to death," the Jews declared. [32] They said this so that Jesus' words might be fulfilled signifying what sort of death He was going to die.

---

[a]18:23 Or him, testify   [b]18:30 Lit an evil doer   [c]18:31 According to Roman law

18:28 This verse does not imply that it was still the day on which the initial evening Passover meal would be eaten. Ritual uncleanness would no longer apply on a new day, and a new day began, in Jewish thinking, at every sundown. Jewish leaders, who were worried about defiling themselves by entering a Gentile home (the palace), must have been concerned about the festive lunch that same day. There is no contradiction with the chronology in the other Gospels.

18:31 It has been argued that the Jews did have the

right to execute capital offenders—witness the stoning of Stephen (Ac 7:54–8:1) and the execution of James the brother of Jesus in A.D. 62 (Josephus, *Antiquities* 20.197-203). But the former execution appears to have degenerated into a mob action and the latter occurred between Roman procurators occupying the government seat in Judea. Josephus's wording also suggests that, in all but a handful of cases, Rome had taken away the privilege of capital punishment (*War* 2.117; 6.124-126).

[33] Then Pilate went back into the headquarters, summoned Jesus, and said to Him, "Are You the King of the Jews?"

[34] Jesus answered, "Are you asking this on your own, or have others told you about Me?"

[35] "I'm not a Jew, am I?" Pilate replied. "Your own nation and the chief priests handed You over to me. What have You done?"

[36] "My kingdom is not of this world," said Jesus. "If My kingdom were of this world, My servants[a] would fight, so that I wouldn't be handed over to the Jews. As it is, My kingdom does not have its origin here."[b]

[37] "You are a king then?" Pilate asked.

"You say that I'm a king," Jesus replied. "I was born for this, and I have come into the world for this: to testify to the truth. Everyone who is of the truth listens to My voice."

[38] "What is truth?" said Pilate.

Jesus or Barabbas

After he had said this, he went out to the Jews again and told them, "I find no grounds for charging Him. [39] You have a custom that I release one ⌊prisoner⌋ to you at the Passover. So, do you want me to release to you the King of the Jews?"

[40] They shouted back, "Not this man, but Barabbas!" Now Barabbas was a revolutionary.[c]

Jesus Flogged and Mocked

19 Then Pilate took Jesus and had Him flogged. [2] The soldiers also twisted together a crown of thorns, put it on His head, and threw a purple robe around Him. [3] And they repeatedly came up to Him and said, "Hail, King of the Jews!" and were slapping His face.

[4] Pilate went outside again and said to them, "Look, I'm bringing Him outside to you to let you know I find no grounds for charging Him."

Pilate Sentences Jesus to Death

[5] Then Jesus came out wearing the crown of thorns and the purple robe. Pilate said to them, "Here is the man!"

[6] When the chief priests and the temple police saw Him, they shouted, "Crucify! Crucify!"

Pilate responded, "Take Him and crucify Him yourselves, for I find no grounds for charging Him."

[7] "We have a law," the Jews replied to him, "and according to that law He must die, because He made Himself[d] the Son of God."

[8] When Pilate heard this statement, he was more afraid than ever. [9] He went back into the headquarters and asked Jesus, "Where are You from?" But Jesus did not give him an answer. [10] So Pilate said to Him, "You're not talking to me? Don't You know that I have the authority to release You and the authority to crucify You?"

[11] "You would have no authority over Me at all," Jesus answered him, "if it hadn't been given you from above. This is why the one who handed Me over to you has the greater sin."[e]

[12] From that moment Pilate made every

---

[a]18:36 Or *attendants*, or *helpers* [b]18:36 Lit *My kingdom is not from here* [c]18:40 Or *robber*; see Jn 10:1,8 for the same Gk word used here [d]19:7 He claimed to be [e]19:11 To *have sin* is an idiom that refers to guilt caused by sin.

18:36 This verse does not mean that Jesus' "kingdom" had no earthly manifestations but that its origin was not of this world.

18:39 Because there is no unambiguous evidence for this "custom" in non-biblical sources, many doubt that it existed. On the other hand, the writings of the Jewish historian Josephus (*Antiquities* 20.209), the Roman historian Livy (5.13), and the rabbinical authors of the Talmud (b. Pes. 91a) may attest to the custom or, more likely, to partially analogous Roman practices, making this biblical account plausible.

19:1 Was Jesus flogged once or twice? Probably only once; He might not even have survived two such punishments. Mark described the incident later in his narrative (Mk 15:15). However, he introduced the incident with "After having Jesus flogged . . . ," allowing for it to have occurred earlier in Jesus' trial.

19:12,15 Jewish authorities were hardly friends of Caesar (v. 12); could they really have affirmed their allegiance to him (v. 15)? Probably only in the sense that they would have said just about anything to get Pilate to crucify Jesus. Pilate would have cared deeply about how the emperor viewed him, so these statements were ploys to get him to look favorably on their request.

effort[a] to release Him. But the Jews shouted, "If you release this man, you are not Caesar's friend. Anyone who makes himself a king opposes Caesar!"

[13] When Pilate heard these words, he brought Jesus outside. He sat down on the judge's bench in a place called the Stone Pavement (but in Hebrew *Gabbatha*). [14] It was the preparation day for the Passover, and it was about six in the morning.[b] Then he told the Jews, "Here is your king!"

[15] But they shouted, "Take Him away! Take Him away! Crucify Him!"

Pilate said to them, "Should I crucify your king?"

"We have no king but Caesar!" the chief priests answered.

[16] So then, because of them, he handed Him over to be crucified.

The Crucifixion

Therefore they took Jesus away.[c] [17] Carrying His own cross, He went out to what is called Skull Place, which in Hebrew is called *Golgotha*. [18] There they crucified Him and two others with Him, one on either side, with Jesus in the middle. [19] Pilate also had a sign lettered and put on the cross. The inscription was:

> **JESUS THE NAZARENE**
> **THE KING OF THE JEWS**

[20] Many of the Jews read this sign, because the place where Jesus was crucified was near the city, and it was written in Hebrew,[d] Latin, and Greek. [21] So the chief priests of the Jews said to Pilate, "Don't write, 'The King of the Jews,' but that He said, 'I am the King of the Jews.' "

[22] Pilate replied, "What I have written, I have written."

[23] When the soldiers crucified Jesus, they took His clothes and divided them into four parts, a part for each soldier. They also took the tunic, which was seamless, woven in one piece from the top. [24] So they said to one another, "Let's not tear it, but toss for it, to see who gets it." [They did this] to fulfill the Scripture that says: **They divided My clothes among themselves, and they cast lots for My clothing.**[e] And this is what the soldiers did.

Jesus' Provision for His Mother

[25] Standing by the cross of Jesus were His mother, His mother's sister, Mary the wife of Clopas, and Mary Magdalene. [26] When Jesus saw His mother and the disciple He

---

[a]19:12 Lit *Pilate was trying* [b]19:14 Lit *the sixth hour*; see note at Jn 1:39; an alternate time reckoning would be *about noon* [c]19:16 Other mss add *and led Him out* [d]19:20 Or *Aramaic* [e]19:24 Ps 22:18

19:14,31,42 The Greek of verse 14 reads literally, "Now it was the preparation of the Passover." But in light of verse 31, this must have meant the day of preparation for the Sabbath (i.e., Friday before Saturday) of Passover week. John spoke of the sixth hour, but Mk 15:25 has Jesus on the cross already by the third hour. Some think John was following Roman reckoning of hours, beginning at midnight, and referring to 6:00 A.M., while Mark was following Jewish reckoning, beginning at dawn and thus referring to 9:00 A.M. Others believe both writers were using round numbers, following Jewish reckoning, in a world where the days and nights were often divided into fourths. A midmorning time of roughly 10:30 could then get rounded either down or up to the nearest three-hour marker.

19:17 John said Jesus carried His own cross (as crucified people usually did), but Mk 15:21 describes the authorities conscripting Simon of Cyrene for that task. Presumably, Jesus started out carrying it, but the weight of the wood could have made it difficult for Jesus, weakened by the flogging, to walk far with it.

19:24,36 This is another passage that is typological in the OT (Ps 22:18). Psalm 22 contains numerous details strikingly paralleled in Jesus' life, even though it was originally describing the afflictions of the psalmist. To the believing Jew, this was no coincidence but a sign of God's hand at work

19:25-27 Why would Jesus entrust His mother to "the disciple He loved"—the Apostle John—rather than to her husband, Joseph, or to one of Jesus' half brothers? Presumably because Joseph had died by this time and Jesus' brothers had not yet become His followers. It is possible that John was Jesus' cousin, so they had a biological as well as spiritual relationship. In John's account, Mary and her sister are named as witnesses at the crucifixion. John didn't name Mary's sister, but Mark says that Salome was among the women present. Salome was the mother of Zebedee's sons, James and John (Mk 15:40).

loved standing there, He said to His mother, "Woman, here is your son." [27] Then He said to the disciple, "Here is your mother." And from that hour the disciple took her into his home.

The Finished Work of Jesus

[28] After this, when Jesus knew that everything was now accomplished that the Scripture might be fulfilled, He said, "I'm thirsty!" [29] A jar full of sour wine was sitting there; so they fixed a sponge full of sour wine on hyssop[a] and held it up to His mouth.

[30] When Jesus had received the sour wine, He said, "It is finished!" Then bowing His head, He gave up His spirit.

Jesus' Side Pierced

[31] Since it was the preparation day, the Jews did not want the bodies to remain on the cross on the Sabbath (for that Sabbath was a special[b] day). They requested that Pilate have the men's legs broken and that ₗtheir bodiesⱼ be taken away. [32] So the soldiers came and broke the legs of the first man and of the other one who had been crucified with Him. [33] When they came to Jesus, they did not break His legs since they saw that He was already dead. [34] But one of the soldiers pierced His side with a spear, and at once blood and water came out. [35] He who saw this has testified so that you also may believe. His testimony is true, and he knows he is telling the truth. [36] For these things happened so that the Scripture would be fulfilled: **Not one of His bones will be broken.**[c] [37] Also, another Scripture says: **They will look at the One they pierced.**[d]

Jesus' Burial

[38] After this, Joseph of Arimathea, who was a disciple of Jesus—but secretly because of his fear of the Jews—asked Pilate that he might remove Jesus' body. Pilate gave him permission, so he came and took His body away. [39] Nicodemus (who had previously come to Him at night) also came, bringing a mixture of about 75 pounds[e] of myrrh and aloes. [40] Then they took Jesus' body and wrapped it in linen cloths with the aromatic spices, according to the burial custom of the Jews. [41] There was a garden in the place where He was crucified. A new tomb was in the garden; no one had yet been placed in it. [42] They placed Jesus there because of the Jewish preparation and since the tomb was nearby.

The Empty Tomb

20 On the first day of the week Mary Magdalene came to the tomb early, while it was still dark. She saw that the stone had been removed[f] from the tomb. [2] So she ran to Simon Peter and to the other disciple, the one Jesus loved, and said to them, "They have taken the Lord out of the tomb, and we don't know where they have put Him!"

[3] At that, Peter and the other disciple went out, heading for the tomb. [4] The two were running together, but the other disciple outran Peter and got to the tomb first. [5] Stooping down, he saw the linen cloths lying there, yet he did not go in. [6] Then, following him, Simon Peter came also. He entered the tomb and saw the linen cloths lying there. [7] The wrapping that had been on His head was not

---

[a]19:29 Or *with hyssop* [b]19:31 Lit *great* [c]19:36 Ex 12:46; Nm 9:12; Ps 34:20 [d]19:37 Zch 12:10 [e]19:39 Lit *100 litrai*; a Roman *litrai* = 12 ounces [f]20:1 Lit *She saw the stone removed*

19:39 This is the amount of anointing material that was used at the funeral for a king. Would Joseph and Nicodemus really have brought so much? If they had come to believe Jesus was a true king, then why not?

20:1-2 Who went to the tomb when? All the Gospels agree that Mary Magdalene went along with several other women. She may have run ahead to be the first to see the empty tomb, or else John just didn't mention the other women with her. Verse 2, after all, has Mary

saying, "*We* don't know where they have put Him" (emphasis added). Similarly, she may have been the first to get back to the disciples, or else John simply left out Jesus' first appearance to the women as a group. As for going while it was still dark, this scarcely contradicts Mk 16:2 ("at sunrise"), since the minutes before and after dawn always resemble "twilight"—part dark, part light.

How Should a Christian Deal with Doubt?

by Gary R. Habermas

*D*oubt might be defined as uncertainty regarding God or our relation to Him. Questions arise in many forms, including factual or philosophical issues, assurance, suffering, or unanswered prayer.

Doubt may be divided into three general areas. *Factual doubt* usually raises issues regarding the truth of Christianity. *Emotional doubt* chiefly concerns our moods and feelings, often posing questions pertaining to assurance of salvation. *Volitional doubt* is a category that ranges from weak faith to a lack of motivation to follow the Lord.

Few subjects are characterized by more misunderstandings than this one. Contrary to popular opinion, doubt is not always sin. Neither is it necessarily the opposite of faith nor the product of weak faith. It is experienced by many believers in Scripture, such as Abraham, Job, David, Jeremiah, and John the Baptist. And almost all believers, as well as unbelievers, experience doubt at times. As strange as it seems, doubt can produce positive results, and many doubters are very much in love with the Lord.

The answer to *factual doubt* is the facts. In other words, questions concerning God, Jesus, the Bible, or the resurrection are answered by the data. No other religion can claim the kind of foundation upon which Christianity is based. A frequent mistake made by factual doubters is to confuse disputed areas among Christians (e.g., sovereignty versus free will, the age of the earth, the sign gifts, or eternal security) with the core truths: the deity of Jesus Christ, His death and resurrection. A remedy for this kind of doubt is to start with these basics: "If you confess with your mouth, 'Jesus is Lord,' and believe in your heart that God raised Him from the dead, you will be saved" (Rm 10:9). When we believe these basics, our understanding and appropriation of other doctrines will follow.

Emotional doubt is the most common as well as the most painful variety. Frequently, these doubters repeatedly wonder whether they are saved, while exhibiting signs of their obvious love for the Lord. They often tell themselves that what they most desire is just beyond their grasp—hence their pain. Here the chief issue is not what is being said but the distraught moods in the background. The remedy is to treat the latter.

Many passages in Scripture command us to address our unruly emotions (see Ps 37:7-8; 39:2; 42:5-6,11; 55:4-8,16-17,22; 56:3-4; 94:19). Often we must move from our perspective to God's and replace our uncertain feelings with trust in Him.

For instance, in Philippians 4:6-9, Paul tells us to replace our anxieties with prayer and thanksgiving. The apostle promises peace for those who do so (vv. 6-7). Then he commands us to explicitly change our worrisome thoughts to God's truth (v. 8) and to model ourselves after his pattern, again promising the result of peace (v. 9).

The key is to change how we think and behave. Simply diverting attention from our worries can provide temporary relief. The best response, every single time a doubt arises, is to weed out and correct the improper thought by concentrating on God's truth rather than on our shaky beliefs.

Volitional doubt covers a wide range of uncertainty. The more extreme versions are often characterized by formerly committed believers who now seem not to care anymore. Perhaps they even appear to live no differently from unbelievers. This is probably the most dangerous species of doubt, since the individual may be in danger of turning from the Lord. But how do we motivate someone who does not wish to be energized? Friends and loved ones must get involved.

Any biblical means of stirring the dying embers may be helpful here. In Scripture, probably the most frequently prescribed methods are being convicted of sin (Heb 3:12-13) or being challenged by the truth of heaven. Everyone experiences the lure of living forever (Ec 3:11). Believers more specifically seek heaven (Heb 11:16,35; 13:14). Dozens of times we are challenged to pursue our eternal home, applying its truth deeply to our lives (Mt 6:33). After all, what we do for the Lord after salvation helps determine and shape our capacity for enjoying eternity (Mt 6:19-21; Mk 9:41).

Perhaps the key is to assist the volitional doubter in charging his spiritual batteries. What could be worse than failing the God of the universe and falling short of His kingdom? Conversely, what could be better than living with Him and our believing friends and loved ones for a truly blessed eternity? We need to drive these truths home to those who waver, by the power of the Holy Spirit (Jms 5:19-20; Jd 20-23).

Doubt can sometimes be a positive incentive to change and grow. But other times, intervention is necessary. Members of the body of Christ need to be alert and sensitive, helping each other focus on the Lord and His kingdom.

---

lying with the linen cloths but was folded up in a separate place by itself. ⁸ The other disciple, who had reached the tomb first, then entered the tomb, saw, and believed. ⁹ For they still did not understand the Scripture that He must rise from the dead. ¹⁰ Then the disciples went home again.

Mary Magdalene Sees the Risen Lord

¹¹ But Mary stood outside facing the tomb, crying. As she was crying, she stooped to look into the tomb. ¹² She saw two angels in white sitting there, one at the head and one at the feet, where Jesus' body had been lying. ¹³ They said to her, "Woman, why are you crying?"

"Because they've taken away my Lord," she told them, "and I don't know where they've put Him." ¹⁴ Having said this, she turned around and saw Jesus standing there, though she did not know it was Jesus.

¹⁵ "Woman," Jesus said to her, "why are you crying? Who is it you are looking for?"

Supposing He was the gardener, she replied, "Sir, if you've removed Him, tell me where you've put Him, and I will take Him away."

¹⁶ Jesus said, "Mary."

Turning around, she said to Him in Hebrew, *"Rabbouni!"*ᵃ—which means "Teacher."

¹⁷ "Don't cling to Me," Jesus told her, "for I have not yet ascended to the Father. But

---

ᵃ20:16 *Rabbouni* is also used in Mk 10:51

20:11 Mary obviously went back to the tomb, this time probably alone, for this separate special encounter with Jesus. That so much emphasis is placed on her witness (vv. 2,18) is doubly significant, since women's testimony was not often admitted in ancient law courts. Early Christians, if they were making up a story about Jesus' resurrection, would not likely have had a woman, and especially not one with a history of being demon possessed (Lk 8:2), as their primary witness.

20:12 Matthew referred to "an angel" (Mt 28:2); Mark, to

"a young man" (Mk 16:5); and Luke, to "two men" (Lk 24:4). John harmonized the three accounts. Two angels, appearing like men (as consistently in Scripture), were present. Only one is ever said to speak, so abbreviated accounts could easily have left the second one out. Since no Gospel says that only one angel or man was present, there is no contradiction.

20:17 The Greek reads literally, "Don't touch me," but the sense is "Stop clinging to me." It's not that there was something dangerous about Jesus' body (or that it

go to My brothers and tell them that I am ascending to My Father and your Father—to My God and your God."

[18] Mary Magdalene went and announced to the disciples, "I have seen the Lord!" And she told them what[a] He had said to her.

The Disciples Commissioned

[19] In the evening of that first day of the week, the disciples were ⌊gathered together⌋ with the doors locked because of their fear of the Jews. Then Jesus came, stood among them, and said to them, "Peace to you!" [20] Having said this, He showed them His hands and His side. So the disciples rejoiced when they saw the Lord.

[21] Jesus said to them again, "Peace to you! As the Father has sent Me, I also send you." [22] After saying this, He breathed on them and said,[b] "Receive the Holy Spirit. [23] If you forgive the sins of any, they are forgiven them; if you retain ⌊the sins of⌋ any, they are retained."

Thomas Sees and Believes

[24] But one of the Twelve, Thomas (called "Twin"), was not with them when Jesus came. [25] So the other disciples kept telling him, "We have seen the Lord!"

But he said to them, "If I don't see the mark of the nails in His hands, put my finger into the mark of the nails, and put my hand into His side, I will never believe!"

[26] After eight days His disciples were indoors again, and Thomas was with them. Even though the doors were locked, Jesus came and stood among them. He said, "Peace to you!"

[27] Then He said to Thomas, "Put your finger here and observe My hands. Reach out your hand and put it into My side. Don't be an unbeliever, but a believer."

[28] Thomas responded to Him, "My Lord and my God!"

[29] Jesus said, "Because you have seen Me, you have believed.[c] Those who believe without seeing are blessed."

The Purpose of This Gospel

[30] Jesus performed many other signs in the presence of His disciples that are not written in this book. [31] But these are written so that you may believe Jesus is the Messiah, the Son of God,[d] and by believing you may have life in His name.

Jesus' Third Appearance to the Disciples

21 After this, Jesus revealed Himself again to His disciples by the Sea of Tiberias.[e] He revealed Himself in this way:

---

[a]20:18 Lit these things   [b]20:22 Lit He breathed and said to them   [c]20:29 Or have you believed? (as a question)   [d]20:31 Or that the Messiah, the Son of God, is Jesus   [e]21:1 The Sea of Galilee; Sea of Tiberias is used only in John; Jn 6:1,23

---

was not really a body) but that Jesus had not come back to be with Mary permanently in bodily form. These were temporary appearances en route to His ascension and were not to be prolonged.

20:19-23 Is this John's massively reworked counterpart to Pentecost (Ac 2)? No. Only ten of the disciples were present and nothing "spiritual" happened afterward. They simply went fishing (21:3). More likely, this was a dramatic object lesson or initial bestowal of the Spirit to prepare them for the more dramatic filling that would happen seven weeks later in Jerusalem. The authority He bestowed parallels that given first to Peter (Mt 16:16-19) and then to the Twelve (Mt 18:18). It was fulfilled in the disciples' preaching ministry in Ac. Nothing is taught here about papal infallibility or apostolic succession.

20:25-29 This story depicts Thomas in so poor a light that it was not likely invented by the disciples. It also portrays the disciples cowering behind locked doors for fear of the authorities, hardly in any psychological

frame of mind to receive visions of a resurrected Christ. The text also confirms that Jesus was genuinely, bodily raised from the dead. Two theological themes coalesce: This kind of miracle (or sign) should have been adequate to convince people that Jesus was truly Lord and God (v. 28), and the testimony of the disciples should have been adequate to demonstrate that even without firsthand empirical proof (v. 29).

20:30-31 These verses explain the highly selective nature of this Gospel's contents as well as its purpose. The book is one of testimony to the identity of Jesus as Messiah and divine Son. Because these verses seem like an appropriate ending, some have wondered if chapter 21 was added later as a kind of appendix. But it contains numerous references to "unfinished business" from the rest of the Gospel, and other ancient works also exhibit the phenomenon of seeming to end a little bit before they actually do (cp. the location of the purpose statements in John's other writings—1 Jn 5:13; Rv 22:6).

21:1 Why do we suddenly find the disciples back north

[2] Simon Peter, Thomas (called "Twin"), Nathanael from Cana of Galilee, Zebedee's sons, and two others of His disciples were together.

[3] "I'm going fishing," Simon Peter said to them.

"We're coming with you," they told him. They went out and got into the boat, but that night they caught nothing.

[4] When daybreak came, Jesus stood on the shore. However, the disciples did not know it was Jesus.

[5] "Men,"[a] Jesus called to them, "you don't have any fish, do you?"

"No," they answered.

[6] "Cast the net on the right side of the boat," He told them, "and you'll find some." So they did,[b] and they were unable to haul it in because of the large number of fish. [7] Therefore the disciple, the one Jesus loved, said to Peter, "It is the Lord!"

When Simon Peter heard that it was the Lord, he tied his outer garment around him[c] (for he was stripped) and plunged into the sea. [8] But since they were not far from land (about 100 yards[d] away), the other disciples came in the boat, dragging the net full of fish. [9] When they got out on land, they saw a charcoal fire there, with fish lying on it, and bread.

[10] "Bring some of the fish you've just caught," Jesus told them. [11] So Simon Peter got up and hauled the net ashore, full of large fish—153 of them. Even though there were so many, the net was not torn.

[12] "Come and have breakfast," Jesus told them. None of the disciples dared ask Him, "Who are You?" because they knew it was the Lord. [13] Jesus came, took the bread, and gave it to them. He did the same with the fish.

[14] This was now the third time[e] Jesus appeared[f] to the disciples after He was raised from the dead.

Jesus' Threefold Restoration of Peter

[15] When they had eaten breakfast, Jesus asked Simon Peter, "Simon, son of John,[g] do you love[h] Me more than these?"

"Yes, Lord," he said to Him, "You know that I love You."

"Feed My lambs," He told him.

[16] A second time He asked him, "Simon, son of John, do you love Me?"

"Yes, Lord," he said to Him, "You know that I love You."

"Shepherd My sheep," He told him.

[17] He asked him the third time, "Simon, son of John, do you love Me?"

Peter was grieved that He asked him the third time, "Do you love Me?" He said, "Lord, You know everything! You know that I love You."

"Feed My sheep," Jesus said. [18] "I assure you: When you were young, you would tie your belt and walk wherever you wanted. But when you grow old, you will stretch out your hands and someone else will tie you and carry you where you don't want to go." [19] He said this to signify by what kind of death he

---

[a]21:5 Lit *Children*   [b]21:6 Lit *they cast*   [c]21:7 Lit *he girded his garment*   [d]21:8 Lit *about 200 cubits*   [e]21:14 The other two are in Jn 20:19–29.
[f]21:14 Lit *was revealed* (see v. 1)   [g]21:15–17 Other mss read *Simon, son of Jonah*; Jn 1:42; Mt 16:17   [h]21:15–17 Two synonyms are translated *love* in this conversation: *agapao*, the first 2 times by Jesus (vv. 15–16); and *phileo*, the last time by Jesus (v. 17) and all 3 times by Peter (vv. 15–17). Peter's threefold confession of love for Jesus corresponds to his earlier threefold denial of Jesus; Jn 18:15–18,25–27.

---

in Galilee? One week after the beginning of Passover in Jerusalem, the Feast ended. They were heading home. Matthew and Mark described resurrection appearances only in Galilee; Luke, only in Judea. John recognized that Jesus appeared to His followers in both locations.

21:4-14 Is this a doublet (two stories created from one incident) of Lk 5:1-11? Both were miraculous fish catches, but it makes sense to see them as two separate events. The disciples had abandoned Jesus, so He needed to "re-call" them. What better way than via a miracle resembling the one that led to the original call

of several of them? Verses 15-19 are, after all, clearly about reinstatement.

21:14 But John already narrated four appearances! Presumably the one to Mary didn't count as "to the disciples," which leaves three—on Easter Sunday night (20:19-23), one week later (20:24-29) and now later still in Galilee (21:1-14).

21:18-19 Jesus' cryptic prophecy seems to have been fulfilled when Peter was martyred by crucifixion during Nero's persecutions of A.D. 64 and 68, as attested by early church tradition.

would glorify God.[a] After saying this, He told him, "Follow Me!"

Correcting a False Report

[20] So Peter turned around and saw the disciple Jesus loved following them. ⌊That disciple⌋ was the one who had leaned back against Jesus at the supper and asked, "Lord, who is the one that's going to betray You?" [21] When Peter saw him, he said to Jesus, "Lord—what about him?"

[22] "If I want him to remain until I come," Jesus answered, "what is that to you? As for you, follow Me."

[23] So this report[b] spread to the brothers[c] that this disciple would not die. Yet Jesus did not tell him that he would not die, but, "If I want him to remain until I come, what is that to you?"

Epilogue

[24] This is the disciple who testifies to these things and who wrote them down. We know that his testimony is true.

[25] And there are also many other things that Jesus did, which, if they were written one by one, I suppose not even the world itself could contain the books[d] that would be written.

---

[a]21:19 Jesus predicts that Peter would be martyred. Church tradition says that Peter was crucified upside down. [b]21:23 Lit *this word* [c]21:23 The word *brothers* refers to the whole Christian community. [d]21:25 Lit *scroll*

21:22-23 The dominant early church tradition attests that John was the one disciple who did not die a martyr's death but lived out his life in old age to virtually the end of the first century, ministering in and around Ephesus (including a brief exile in the mid-90s on the island of Patmos, during which he wrote the book of Rv). It is possible that John died shortly after completing a draft of his Gospel and that, because of the misinterpreted report described here, his followers added this closing information by way of clarification.

21:24-25 These verses also read most naturally as an addition of John's followers—note the first person singular and plural pronouns versus the third-person reference to the beloved disciple. At the same time they attribute the book itself to John and certify its accuracy. If this reconstruction is accurate, it means merely that God inspired multiple authors, no differently than with the books of Ps or Pr or with the addition of the account of Moses' death to Dt.

THE PLAN OF SALVATION

What do you understand it takes for a person to go to Heaven?
Consider how the Bible answers this question: It's a matter of **FAITH**

F is for FORGIVENESS

We cannot have eternal life and heaven without God's forgiveness.

—Read Ephesians 1:7a.

A is for AVAILABLE

Forgiveness is available. It is—

- Available for all.   —Read John 3:16.
- But not automatic.   —Read Matthew 7:21a.

I is for IMPOSSIBLE

It is impossible for God to allow sin into heaven.

- Because of who He is: God is loving and just.
  His judgment is against sin.   —Read James 2:13a.
- Because of who we are:
  Every person is a sinner.   —Read Romans 3:23.

But how can a sinful person enter heaven, when God allows no sin?

T is for TURN

Turn means to repent.

- Turn from something—sin and self.   —Read Luke 13:3b.
- Turn to Someone; trust Christ only.   —Read Romans 10:9.

H is for HEAVEN

Heaven is eternal life.

- Here   —Read John 10:10b.
- Hereafter   —Read John 14:3

How can a person have God's forgiveness, heaven and eternal life, and Jesus as personal Savior and Lord? By trusting in Christ and asking Him for forgiveness. Take the step of faith described by another meaning of FAITH: Forsaking All I Trust Him.

Prayer:

Lord Jesus, I know I am a sinner and have displeased You in many ways. I believe You died for my sin and only through faith in Your death and resurrection can I be forgiven.

I want to turn from my sin and ask You to come into my life as my Savior and Lord. From this day on, I will follow You by living a life that pleases you. Thank You, Lord Jesus for saving me. Amen.

After you have received Jesus Christ into your life, tell a Christian friend about this important decision you have made. Follow Christ in believer's baptism and church membership. Grow in your faith and enjoy new friends in Christ by becoming part of His church. There, you'll find others who will love and support you.

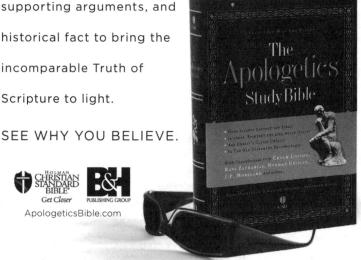